DEIFICATION AND GRACE

INTRODUCTIONS TO CATHOLIC DOCTRINE

This series provides readable scholarly introductions to key themes in Catholic doctrine, written by preeminent scholars from around the world. The volumes of the series are suitable for college, university, and seminary courses, as well as for educated readers of all ages who seek to grow in their understanding of the Catholic faith.

PUBLISHED VOLUMES

Avery Cardinal Dulles, SJ, *Magisterium, Teacher and Guardian of the Faith*
Daniel A. Keating, *Deification and Grace*
Steven A. Long, *The Teleological Grammar of the Moral Object*
Charles Morerod, OP, *The Church and the Human Quest for Truth*
Kenneth Whitehead, *The Renewed Church*

Deification and Grace

Daniel A. Keating

Sapientia Press
of Ave Maria University

14 3

Sapientia Press
of Ave Maria University
1025 Commons Circle
Naples, FL 34119

Cover Image:
Titian (Tiziano Vecellio) (ca.1488–1576)
The Pentecost
S. Maria della Salute, Venice, Italy
Photo: Scala/Art Resource, NY

Cover Design: Eloise Anagnost

Printed in the United States of America.

Library of Congress Control Number: 2006940460

ISBN-10: 1-932589-37-6

ISBN-13: 978-1-932589-37-5

To my brothers in the
Servants of the Word

Table of Contents

Acknowledgments

I OWE a debt of gratitude to my brother, Fr. Michael Keating, and to my colleagues and friends from Oxford, Fr. Tom Weinandy and Dr. John Yocum, for reading through each chapter of the manuscript and offering important corrections and wise suggestions for improvement. I am grateful to Diane Eriksen and her team of editors at Sapientia Press for greatly improving the clarity and comprehensibility of the text. And I am especially thankful for the initiative taken by Dr. Matthew Levering, who proposed that I write on this subject for Sapientia Press and encouraged me heartily along the way.

CHAPTER ONE

The Topic of Christian Deification

What is this advance that is spoken of other than . . . the deification and grace imparted by Wisdom to men?

—Athanasius of Alexandria, *C. Ar.* 3.53

THE CHRISTIAN doctrine of deification (or divinization) certainly needs explaining. While this is true of every Christian doctrine, it is especially true of this one. It is simply not evident to most people what "deification" means. Not only is this term absent from the Bible, but it rings in many ears with overtones of ancient pagan religious practice or philosophical speculation. What place does it have—or should it be granted—in Christian theology? Does it have any bearing on how we are to believe and live as Christians?

When the topic of Christian deification is raised, people typically respond in one of three ways. The first is simple surprise and puzzlement at an unfamiliar and strange-sounding term. What could deification mean for Christian faith and life? While I was working on this study, a student of mine approached me after class, pointed to a paragraph in the *Catechism of the Catholic Church* that speaks of deification, and bluntly asked, "What does this mean?" This is perhaps the most typical response people make when confronted with the notion of deification. The second response is fascination. Having heard distant reports or received short snippets of explanation about deification, these people are intrigued by this exotic-sounding idea and are anxious to hear more. The third response is marked by a knowing frown, and is often followed by a strongly expressed conviction as to why deification is foreign to true, biblical Christianity. This short volume is written to address—though it may not fully satisfy—the audiences that are represented by these three responses.

RENEWED INTEREST IN THE CHRISTIAN DOCTRINE OF DEIFICATION

In the past two or three generations a conscious effort has been made across the Christian spectrum to retrieve an understanding of Christian life in terms of "deification" and to give explicit attention to its meaning and content. Theologians from the Eastern Orthodox churches have—unsurprisingly—been in the forefront of efforts to recapture and re-explain the centrality of *theosis* (the preferred Eastern Orthodox term) for the Christian life.[1] The doctrine of deification functions centrally in Eastern Orthodox theology and liturgy, and it is within the ambit of Orthodoxy that deification *(theosis)* has received its fullest development. Catholic theologians, however, have not been far behind in their efforts to reinvigorate the idea of deification within a specifically Western context.[2] One of the fruits of this retrieval can be

1 Vladimir Lossky (d. 1958) gives notable attention to deification *(theosis)* in *The Mystical Theology of the Eastern Church* (Cambridge: James Clarke, 1991), and *In the Image and Likeness of God* (Crestwood, NY: St. Vladimir's Press, 1974). Norman Russell, *The Doctrine of Deification,* 316–17, identifies the 1960s as the turning point for Orthodox theology toward the recovery of the Palamite doctrine of *theosis.* Among prominent Orthodox theologians since the 1960s who have written on deification are: John Meyendorff, *Byzantine Theology* (New York: Fordham University Press, 1974), 163–65; Christoforos Stavropoulos, *Partakers of the Divine Nature,* trans. Stanley Harakas (Minneapolis: Light and Life, 1976); Kallistos Ware, "Salvation and Theosis in Orthodox Theology," in W. Schneemelcher, ed., *Luther et la réforme allemande dans une perspective oecuménique* (Geneva: Éditions du Centre Orthodoxe, 1983), 167–84; G. I. Mantzaridis, *The Deification of Man: St. Gregory Palamas and the Orthodox Tradition,* trans. Liadain Sherrard (Crestwood, NY: St. Vladimir's Press, 1984); John Zizioulas, *Being as Communion* (Crestwood, NY: St. Vladimir's Press, 1985); P. Nellas, *Deification in Christ: Perspectives on the Nature of the Human Person,* trans. Norman Russell (Crestwood, NY: St. Vladimir's Press, 1987).

2 In a landmark article drawing on the research of M. Lot-Borodine, Yves Congar, "La déification dans le tradition spirituelle de l'Orient," *La vie spirituelle,*

found in the 1994 publication of the *Catechism of the Catholic Church* (second edition, 1997). The article on the Incarnation (§460), while not using the term "deification" explicitly, cites 2 Peter 1:4 (an important text for deification), and makes reference to the classic patristic formula that lies at the root of the doctrine of deification:

> The Word became flesh to make us *"partakers of the divine nature"* (2 Pet 1:4): "For this is why the Word became man, and the Son of God became the Son of man: so that man, by entering into communion with the Word and thus receiving divine sonship, might become a son of God" [Irenaeus]. "For the Son of God became man so that we might become God" [Athanasius]. "The only-begotten Son of God, wanting to make us sharers in his divinity, assumed our nature, so that he, made man, might make men gods" [Thomas Aquinas].[3]

It is noteworthy, though, that the *Catechism* does not explain what all this means—it relies largely on simple citation. And when it does use the term "divinize," it supplies no definition of the meaning of this term.[4]

---

43 (1935), suppl., 91–107, compares the Eastern and Western traditions, and recommends a recapturing of the riches of the East by the West. Jules Gross provides a rigorous historical study of the doctrine of deification in the East: *La divinisation du chrétien d'après les Pères grecs* (Paris: Gabalda, 1938); English translation: *The Divinization of the Christian according to the Greek Fathers,* trans. Paul A. Onica (Anaheim: A & C Press, 2002). Louis Bouyer is notable for his efforts to translate the notion of deification into Western terms: *The Christian Mystery: From Pagan Myth to Christian Mysticism,* trans. I. Trethowan (Edinburgh: T&T Clark, 1989). Russell, *The Doctrine of Deification,* 315–16, states that the prominent Catholic theologians Karl Rahner and Hans Urs von Balthasar teach the essence of deification without making much use of the vocabulary.

3 See John Paul II, General Audience, May 27, 1998, for a commentary on this paragraph of the *Catechism.* John Paul cites 2 Pet 1:4 and these citations from the Fathers as an answer to the question, What was the Holy Spirit's purpose in bringing about the event of the Incarnation?

4 In the *Catechism* §398, man in original innocence is said to be in a state of holiness and "destined to be fully 'divinized' by God in glory," but we are not told what this divinization (either partial or full) entails. On three occasions, the term "divinize" is found in citations of the Greek Fathers, without further explanation (§1589, Gregory of Nazianzus states that the priest of Christ is "divinized and divinizes"; §1988, Athanasius links our divinization with the gift

It is perhaps no great surprise that the doctrine of deification has received renewed attention in Orthodox and even Catholic circles. What is more striking is the interest that some theologians from the churches of the Reformation are giving to the notion of deification. Anglican writers, especially those steeped in patristic theology, have long been well-disposed to the idea of deification.[5] But now we have a school of Lutheran theology that claims to find a form of deification within Luther's own theology of the Cross, and others find evidence for a doctrine of deification, for example, in John Calvin and John Wesley.[6] Given this widespread interest in deification from various

---

of the indwelling Spirit; §2670, Gregory of Nazianzus claims that we are divinized by the Spirit in baptism). The fullest sense of deification appears in §1999, where the grace of Christ is identified as "the *sanctifying* or *deifying* grace received in Baptism" (emphasis in original). Here deification is placed in parallel with sanctification, and located at the point of baptism. As we shall see, this is just how the Fathers of the Church most commonly locate and understand deification.

5 A. M. Allchin, *Participation in God: A Forgotten Strand in Anglican Tradition* (Wilton, CT: Morehouse-Barlow, 1988). For the influence of the Greek Fathers and the doctrine of deification on the Anglican Oxford Movement, see Andrew Louth, "Manhood into God: the Oxford Movement, the Fathers and the Deification of Man," in *Essays Catholic and Radical*, ed. Kenneth Leech and Rowan Williams (London: Bowerdean, 1983), 70–80. The theology of deification also shows up prominently in the work of twentieth-century Anglican theologian-philosopher E. L. Mascall: *Christ, the Christian and the Church: A Study of the Incarnation and its Consequences* (London: Longmans, Green and Co., 1946).

6 Veli-Matti Kärkkäinen, *One With God: Salvation as Deification and Justification* (Collegeville, MN: Liturgical Press, 2004), outlines the Lutheran renewal of interest in deification, and points to the broad attestation to deification in Anabaptist authors. For a study of the rediscovery of deification in Luther, see Carl E. Braaten and Robert W. Jenson, eds., *Union with Christ: The New Finnish Interpretation of Luther* (Grand Rapids, MI: Eerdmans, 1998). For deification in Calvin, see Carl Mosser, "The Greatest Possible Blessing: Calvin and Deification," *Scottish Journal of Theology* 55 (2002): 367. For aspects of deification in Wesley, see Steve K. McCormick, "Theosis in Chrysostom and Wesley: An Eastern Paradigm on Faith and Love," *Wesleyan Theological Journal* 26 (1991): 38–103, and Michael J. Christensen, "Theosis and Sanctification: John Wesley's Reformulation of a Patristic Doctrine," *Wesleyan Theological Journal* 31 (1996): 71–94. For an evangelical account of deification, see Robert V. Rakestraw, "Becoming like God: An Evangelical Doctrine of Theosis," *Journal of Evangelical Theology*, 40 (1997): 257–69.

theological perspectives and commitments, there is need for a clear description of what the classical Christian doctrine of deification is, and an estimation of what value it may possess.

Aim and Scope of This Study

My aim in this volume is modest. I hope to present—in summary form—a synthetic account of deification in Christ as the full outworking of grace in the Christian life. The topic of "grace" in general is far beyond the scope of what can be addressed here. This is not a treatise on grace as such, but rather an account of grace in terms of our deification in Christ through the Spirit.

Toward this end, I will draw selectively upon the substantial scholarship on deification that has appeared in recent years, including biblical exegesis, historical surveys, terminological studies, and ecumenical comparisons. But I cannot hope to cover all the analytical, historical, and comparative ground in any detail. My limited purpose, rather, is to offer a theological account of deification in summary form, so that readers may grasp its essential elements and understand how deification offers an integrated account of the Christian understanding of salvation.

Certain convictions guide and motivate this effort. The first is that the doctrine of deification is (and must be) grounded in and closely aligned with the Scripture. Deification in its fundamental form emerged not primarily as a speculative exercise aimed at harmonizing Greek thought with Christian faith, but as the expression of Christian belief in the face of various unorthodox accounts that threatened that faith. It was the Gnostic challenge of the second and third centuries, and the Arian crisis of the fourth, that gave rise to the classic concepts and language of deification. In other words, the doctrine of deification arose from the Church's hard-fought efforts to interpret the Scriptures rightly in the face of alternative interpretations of those same Scriptures.

A second conviction, closely related to the first, is that the doctrine of deification is not the patrimony of the Eastern church alone, or an eccentricity of certain schools of Western theology.[7] Rather,

[7] Kärkkäinen, *One With God,* 1, concurs: "Even though the Eastern wing of the church has been the major carrier of this doctrine through the patristic era to our days, never has it been the sole treasure of one part of Christendom."

deification concerns the basic economy of God in Christ through the Spirit that is at the patristic root of both the Eastern and Western theological traditions.[8] As a Catholic raised in the Western tradition and familiar with the Latin Church Fathers, I have also studied certain of the Greek Fathers extensively and have benefited from the wider Byzantine tradition. One goal of this work is to show the remarkable convergence on the substance of the doctrine of deification between the Eastern and Western traditions. This aim in no way denies real differences, large and small, that exist between authors and their respective accounts of deification. By proposing that there is a core account of deification common to many writers in the Christian tradition, I am not seeking to flatten the differences. Each author, and each theological tradition, possesses peculiar elements. These are worthy of sustained attention, but they are not the focus of this study.[9]

---

8 Gösta Hallonsten, "*Theosis* in Recent Research: A Renewal of Interest and a Need for Clarity," in *Partakers of the Divine Nature: The History and Development of Deification in the Christian Traditions*, eds. Michael J. Christensen and Jeffrey A. Wittung (Madison/Teaneck, NJ: Fairleigh Dickinson University Press, 2007), 281–93, cautions against speaking of a "doctrine" of deification in a general sense. He argues that the tendency to find a doctrine of deification in the West (whether in Augustine, Aquinas, or Luther) often obscures what is unique about the Eastern Orthodox doctrine of deification, namely, its comprehensive sense that includes a distinctive theological anthropology and encompasses the whole economy of salvation. He recommends that we speak of a "theme" of deification to describe the more generic sense of deification found throughout the Christian tradition, East and West, and that we reserve the phrase "doctrine of deification" for the more comprehensive Eastern account, grounded in an anthropology of image and likeness. He is certainly correct in identifying distinctive features of the Eastern account. The various accounts of deification from across the Christian spectrum are similar, not identical. Yet he does name Irenaeus as the founder of the doctrine of *theosis*, and it is the very Irenaean account of the economy of salvation that (I shall argue) is found substantially in key Western Fathers and Aquinas. To describe this simply as a "theme" is insufficient. This account of deification, even when it differs from the Eastern one in certain respects, provides something of a theological framework for Western writers, even when its potential is not as fully explored and exploited as it is in the East. The term "doctrine" need not mean a highly developed and systematic account. It can also more simply point to a "teaching" that gives important shape to Christian theology. It is in this sense that I employ the phrase "doctrine of deification" here.

9 For a typology of different accounts of deification in the patristic period, see Russell, *The Doctrine of Deification,* 1–15.

A third conviction that guides this work is that a theological account of Christian deification must be firmly embedded within classical Christian doctrine and the creedal confession of the Church. Deification is not something unto itself, and does not stand alone. It needs to be understood in close correlation with justification, sanctification, filial adoption, regeneration, grace-filled union, transformation, and so forth. Deification is a kind of summary term that expresses all that God intends for us in Christ through the Spirit.

As a consequence of these three convictions—that deification is a "catholic" doctrine of the East and West, grounded in the Scriptures, and embedded within Christian doctrine—the testimony of the Church Fathers will be the center of gravity of this study. Though I will also call upon medieval and modern witnesses, I will rely most heavily on the testimony of the Fathers of the Church. The doctrine of deification emerged in the patristic period as the Fathers wrestled with the Scriptures to understand rightly the doctrine of salvation in Christ. It is to our benefit to have that testimony made more readily available.

Key Questions to Address

There are certain questions that, like a besieging army at the walls, recurrently beset the doctrine of deification. The first we have already identified. Is the doctrine of deification as classically formulated really a biblical doctrine at all, or is it not rather an import from Greek thought foreign to true Christianity, that like a persistent weed refuses to die out? A second question worries about an overemphasis on the Incarnation in the classic formulation of deification. By so magnifying the importance of the Word becoming flesh in the Incarnation, does not deification ignore (or at least minimize) the reality of sin and the need for redemption through Christ's sacrificial death on the Cross? In other words, does this doctrine sidestep the centrality of Christ's atoning death? A third query concerns the distinction between God and creation. Doesn't the doctrine of deification, by virtue of its elevated and exaggerated rhetoric, effectively compromise the fundamental distinction between God and the created order, and so lead explicitly or implicitly to a form of pantheism? Finally, the question gets raised about the overall warrant and usefulness of the doctrine of deification. Is it permissible and warranted, given the objections raised above? And if so, is it really useful? Does it add anything to our grasp of the saving work of God in Christ, or does it just provide a largely poetic metaphor of our salvation at the high cost of potentially confusing and exaggerating the Christian Gospel?

Though the chief purpose of this volume is to present a summary theological account of the Christian doctrine of deification, these questions will be considered en route and will be directly addressed in the conclusions. If we are to understand deification and appreciate its value as expressive of Christian truth, we have to address directly and fairly the recurring concerns and misrepresentations that arise.

NOTE ON TERMINOLOGY

The Christian doctrine of deification is joined to and expressed by a distinctive vocabulary that appeared first in the Greek Fathers and was then translated into Latin. The most common early terms, found in the Alexandrian Fathers (Clement, Origen, Athanasius, and Cyril), are *theopoieō* (to deify/divinize) and *theopoiēsis* (deification/divinization). Following the usage of Gregory of Nazianzus, these terms were largely replaced in the Byzantine tradition by the terms *theoō* (to deify/divinize) and *theōsis* (deification/divinization), the latter term coined by Gregory himself.[10] The Greek terms were translated by the Latin *deificare* (to deify/divinize) and *deificatus* (deified/divinized), which appear, for example, in the writings of Augustine and Thomas Aquinas.

It is crucial, however, to recognize a distinction between the content of the doctrine of deification and its characteristic vocabulary. On the one hand the content of deification may be present in the absence of the technical vocabulary, while on the other the vocabulary may be used with only some marginal aspect of the doctrine in view. The terminology is significant, and it does signal to us that an author has some concept of deification in view, but it is not required for us to recognize the content of the doctrine. In other words, we cannot simply follow a terminological trail in order to discover what the content

[10] For a detailed historical survey of the Greek terminology of deification in pagan, Jewish, and Christian sources, see Russell, *The Doctrine of Deification,* 333–44.

of this doctrine is. Once we grasp what the essential meaning of deification is, we can identify its content even when the vocabulary is absent. Irenaeus of Lyons (second century), for example, never employs the characteristic vocabulary of deification, but he is rightly credited with being the originator of the doctrine of deification in Christ through the Spirit.[11] Likewise, Leo the Great (d. 461) never uses the terminology, but he is one of the clearest exponents of the content of the doctrine of divinization in the Western tradition.[12] One goal of this study, then, is to clarify the *content* of the Christian doctrine of deification, so that when we as readers encounter its characteristic terminology, we will have a clearer understanding of what that terminology means.

---

11 Basil Studer, "Divinization," *Encyclopedia of the Early Church,* vol. 1, ed. Angelo Di Berardino, trans. Adrian Walford (New York: Oxford University Press, 1992), states that "Irenaeus worked out [in response to gnostic ideas] the first authentically Christian synthesis of man's divinization." Russell, *The Doctrine of Deification,* 105, observes that Irenaeus does not use the characteristic vocabulary of deification, but that nonetheless "he presents a 'realist' account of salvation which will provide a number of later writers—Athanasius in particular—with the content of their doctrine of deification."

12 For a study of Leo the Great's theology in terms of "salvation as divinization," see Daniel A. Keating, *The Appropriation of Divine Life in Cyril of Alexandria* (Oxford: Oxford University Press, 2004), 251–88.

CHAPTER TWO

The Graced Exchange: Redeemed Humanity in Christ

For since he bestowed on us his own image and his own Spirit and we did not keep them safe, he took himself a share in our poor and weak nature, in order that he might cleanse us and make us incorruptible, and establish us once more as partakers of his divinity

—John of Damascus, *De Fid. Orth.* 4.13

THE FORMULA OF EXCHANGE IN THE TRADITION

THERE IS no better place to begin a study of deification than with what is commonly termed the "formula of exchange" (often designated in the Christian tradition as the *admirabile commercium*). In essence, this formula states that the eternal Son of God became what we are so that we could become what he is. There is no single established formula—each author who employs this paradoxical expression devises his own version. The earliest examples come from Irenaeus, who is considered the originator of this way of summarizing our redemption.

> For it was for this end that the Word of God was made man, and he who was the Son of God became the Son of man, that man, having been taken into the Word, and receiving the adoption, might become the son of God.[1]

---

[1] *Adv. Haer.* 3. 19. 1; Ante-Nicene Fathers (hereafter ANF), vol. 1 (reprint, Grand Rapids, MI: Eerdmans, 1975), 448. Following the language of the Bible and the Fathers, I will often use the terms "sons" and "sonship" when describing our deification. In every case, "sons" means "sons and daughters"—there is no distinction between male and female in terms of our inheritance in Christ and our call to deification.

> But [we follow] the only true and steadfast Teacher, the Word of God, our Lord Jesus Christ, who did, through his transcendent love, become what we are, that he might bring us to be even what he is Himself.[2]

Norman Russell identifies this Irenaean principle as the "fundamental tenet" of the Christian doctrine of deification.[3] Gerald Bonner likewise claims that the declaration that the Son became man that we might become gods "teaches deification without actually employing the word."[4] Hans Urs von Balthasar identifies the formula of exchange as the "fundamental approach" to the doctrine of salvation found in the Fathers.[5]

Following Irenaeus—and probably dependent upon him—we find wide attestation to this formula throughout the patristic period. It is noteworthy that some form of this expression can be found in writers from Alexandria, Constantinople, Antioch, Syria, North Africa, and Rome. A selection of these witnesses, varying widely in expression, will show how widespread was this manner of summing up the Christian faith.

Clement of Alexandria (third century) writes that "the Word of God became man, that you may learn from man how man may become God."[6] Athanasius of Alexandria (fourth century) made the formula of exchange of key part of his anti-Arian theology: "For he was made man that we might be made God," and "he himself has made us sons of the Father, and deified men by becoming himself man."[7] From the Cappadocian Fathers (fourth century) we hear the same message. Gregory of Nazianzus exhorts his hearers: "Let us become as Christ is,

---

2 *Adv. Haer.* 5. praef.; ANF, vol. 1, 526.

3 Russell, *The Doctrine of Deification,* 321.

4 "Augustine's Conception of Deification," *Journal of Theological Studies,* New Series 37 (1986): 369.

5 *Theo-Drama: Theological Dramatic Theory,* vol. 4, trans. Graham Harrison (San Francisco, CA: Ignatius Press, 1994), 244.

6 *Protr.* 1; ANF, vol. 2, 174.

7 *De Incar.* 54; A Select Library of the Nicene and Post-Nicene Fathers of the Christian Church (hereafter NPNF), 2nd series, vol. 4, 65; *C. Arian.* 1. 38; NPNF, 2nd series, vol. 4, 329.

since Christ became as we are; let us become gods for his sake, since he became man for our sake."[8] Gregory of Nyssa says that the Word became incarnate "so that by becoming as we are, he might make us as he is."[9] In the late fourth century, the Antiochene John Chrysostom teaches that "he became Son of man, who was God's own Son, in order that he might make the sons of men to be children of God."[10] And Ephrem the Syrian (fourth century) adds his own terse formulation of this truth: "He gave us divinity, we gave him humanity."[11]

The formula of exchange is widely attested also in the West. Hilary of Poitiers (fourth century) offers his own twist on this expression: "For when God was born to be man the purpose was not that the Godhead should be lost, but that, the Godhead remaining, man should be born to be god."[12] Ambrose of Milan (fourth century) also utilizes the exchange formula to show how the eternal Son became what he was not in order to bring us to what he was:

> For [the Son] took on him that which he was not that he might hide that which he was; he hid that which he was that he might be tempted in it, and that which he was not might be redeemed, in order that he might call us by means of that which he was not to that which he was.[13]

Augustine employs some form of this expression on numerous occasions. "God wanted to be the Son of Man and he wanted men to be the

---

8 *Or.* 1. 5; trans. Russell, *The Doctrine of Deification,* 215.

9 *Antirrh.* 11; trans. Russell, *The Doctrine of Deification,* 229.

10 *Hom. Io.* 11. 1; NPNF, 1st series, vol. 14, 38.

11 *H. de Fid.* 5:7; cited in Russell, *The Doctrine of Deification,* 322. The *Macarian Homilies* (early fifth-century Syriac) also employ a version of the formula of exchange: "The infinite, inaccessible, and uncreated God . . . has assumed a body . . . so as to be able to be united with his visible creatures . . . so they can be made participators of divine life (2 Pet. 1:4)" (*Hom.* 4. 9). *Pseudo-Macarius: The Fifty Spiritual Homilies and the Great Letter,* trans. and ed. George A. Maloney (Mahwah, NJ: Paulist, 1992), 54.

12 *De. Trin.* 10. 7; NPNF, 2nd series, vol. 9, 183–84. Cf. Hilary's statement in *De Trin.* 9. 4: "The assumption of our nature was no advancement for God, but His willingness to lower Himself is our promotion, for He did not resign His divinity but conferred divinity on man" (156).

13 *De. Spir.* I. 9. 107; NPNF, 2nd series, vol. 10, 107.

sons of God."[14] "The Son of God [became] the Son of man that he might make the sons of men the sons of God."[15] "For this thing God does, out of sons of men he makes sons of God: because out of Son of God he has made Son of Man. . . . For the Son of God has been made partaker of mortality, in order that mortal man may be made partaker of divinity."[16] Pope Leo the Great (fifth century), for whom the formula of exchange was exceedingly important, adds the testimony of Rome: "[The Savior] was made the son of man, so that we could be the sons of God." "He united humanity to himself in such a way that he remained God, unchangeable. He imparted divinity to human beings in such a way that he did not destroy, but enriched them, by glorification."[17]

Witness to this formula appears also in the writings of major theologians, both East and West, of later centuries. In the East, Maximus the Confessor (seventh century) eloquently expresses the content of this formula: "For through the perfect recovery of nature you are distinguished by grace alone and are destined by the power that derives from this to be proved a god in the same degree as he who is God by nature partook of our weakness when he became incarnate."[18] John of Damascus (seventh–eighth centuries) sums up salvation history by means of this formula: "For since he bestowed on us his own image and his own Spirit and we did not keep them safe, he took himself a share in our poor and weak nature, in order that he might cleanse us and make us incorruptible, and establish us once more as partakers of his divinity."[19] Symeon the New Theologian (tenth–eleventh centuries) crisply sums up this truth: "Why did God become man? So that man might become god."[20] And Thomas Aquinas (thirteenth century) shows that this formula was alive and well in the Latin Middle Ages:

---

14 *Trac. in Io.* 12. 8; St. Augustine, *Tractates on the Gospel of John 11–27,* trans. John W. Rettig, Fathers of the Church, vol. 79 (Washington, DC: Catholic University of America Press, 1988), 36.

15 *Trac. in Io.* 21. 1; Rettig, vol. 79, 179.

16 *Enar. in Ps.* 52. 5; NPNF, 1st series, vol. 8, 204, adjusted.

17 *Serm.* 26. 2 (translation by author); 91. 2; *St. Leo the Great: Sermons,* trans. Jane P. Freeland and Agnes J. Conway, Fathers of the Church, vol. 93 (Washington, DC: Catholic University of America Press, 1996), 384.

18 *Amb. Th.* 3; trans. Russell, *The Doctrine of Deification,* 283.

19 *De Fid. Orth.* 4. 13; NPNF, 1st series, vol. 11, 82.

20 *Eth.* 5. 31–4; trans. Russell, *The Doctrine of Deification,* 301.

> The only-begotten Son of God, wishing to make us sharers in his divine nature, assumed our nature, so that made man he might make men gods.[21]
>
> For the human mind and will could never imagine, understand or ask that God become man, and that man become God and a sharer in the divine nature. But he has done this in us by his power, and it was accomplished in the Incarnation of his Son: "That you may become partakers of the divine nature" (2 Pet 1:4).[22]

The formula of exchange is not lacking in the works of the Protestant Reformers. In a Christmas sermon for 1514, Martin Luther writes: "For the Word becomes flesh precisely so that the flesh may become word. In other words: God becomes man so that man may become God."[23] John Calvin gives eloquent expression to this exchange by drawing out the various ways in which the grace of God in Christ has enriched us:

> This is the wonderful exchange which, out of his measureless benevolence, he has made with us; that, by his descent to earth, he has prepared an ascent to heaven for us; that, by taking on our mortality, he has conferred his immortality upon us; that, accepting our weakness, he has strengthened us by his power; that, receiving our poverty unto himself, he has transferred his wealth to us; that, taking the weight of our iniquity upon himself (which oppressed us), he has clothed us with his righteousness.[24]

---

21 *Opusc.* 57; trans. Andrew Louth, "Manhood into God," 74.

22 *In Eph.* 3:19 [182]; Thomas Aquinas, *Commentary on Saint Paul's Epistle to the Ephesians,* trans. and intro. Matthew L. Lamb (Albany, NY: Magi, 1966), 147. Regarding Aquinas and deification, Fergus Kerr, *After Aquinas: Versions of Thomism* (Oxford: Blackwell, 2002), writes: "If [Thomas] was economical with the word ["deifies"], he nevertheless had a rich conception of the transforming effect of divine grace on the individual believer which clearly amounts to the traditional patristic doctrine of deification" (149). "Thomas maintains the patristic doctrine of sanctification as deification . . . and surely should be read in the light of his commitment to the doctrine of deification" (161). See especially Kerr's chapter 9, "Deified Creaturehood."

23 *Weimarer Ausgabe* 1, 28, 25–32; cited in Kärkkäinen, *One With God,* 47.

24 *Institutes* 4. 17. 2; cited in Mosser, "The Greatest Possible Blessing," 44.

Joseph Ratzinger (Pope Benedict XVI) provides us with a contemporary restatement of this exchange at the heart of the Gospel: "This exchange consists of God taking our human existence on himself in order to bestow his divine existence on us, of his choosing our nothingness in order to give his plenitude."[25]

It is crucial to recognize that the formula of exchange, in the variety of its expressions, is a shorthand way to sum up all that God has done in Christ for the human race. It is a pithy and paradoxical statement intended to display at once the marvelous condescension of the Son of God and the wonderful destiny to which he has called us in himself. But what *exactly* does it mean? Is it just the invention of the Fathers, or does it have a sound biblical grounding? What does it entail and what does it exclude? If we as modern readers are to make sense of the formula of exchange and grasp why so many early Christian teachers employed it as a summary of our redemption in Christ, we need to investigate its biblical foundations and rediscover the theological narrative that it encapsulates.

THE BIBLICAL GROUNDING FOR THE FORMULA OF EXCHANGE

2 Corinthians 8:9. A single verse, embedded in Paul's exhortation to the Corinthians on generosity, will serve as a starting point. In 2 Corinthians 8:9, Paul writes: "For you know the grace of our Lord Jesus Christ, that for your sake he became poor, though being rich, so that by his poverty you may become rich."[26] Paul assumes in this text that they know the "grace" of Jesus Christ toward them, that he became something he was not (that is, poor), so that by this poverty we might become something he is, but that we were not (that is, rich). The Fathers justifiably read this text in the light of Philippians 2:5–11. On this reading, "being rich" (2 Cor 8:9) is equivalent to "being in the form of God" (Phil 2:6)—and the present tense of the participle in both verses underscored for the Fathers that the Son of God *remained* God and *retained* his riches, even in the act of emptying himself and

[25] *Dogma and Preaching,* trans. Matthew J. O'Connell (Chicago, IL: Franciscan Herald Press, 1985), 84.

[26] Translation by the author. Unless otherwise noted, translations of the Bible are from the Revised Standard Version (RSV).

becoming poor. Indeed, the exchange at the heart of both these texts makes no sense if Christ, in his condescension, loses the very thing he came to bring us. In the same way, "he became poor" is equivalent to "emptied himself . . . was born . . . and became obedient to death" (Phil 2:7–8). It is shorthand for Christ's Incarnation, passion, and death. But the key difference between the two texts appears at this point. In Philippians 2, the climax reached is the exaltation of the Son himself in his resurrection and enthronement as Lord above all creatures. In 2 Corinthians 8, the climactic result is *our* enrichment. By means of the Son's humbling of himself, we are enriched with his own riches. Though the details of this enrichment are not specified here, this verse, with its paradoxical expressions, indicates a kind of uneven exchange at the heart of our redemption. The Son of God assumed the poverty of our fallen humanity, so that we might be enriched by his redemption of that humanity.

Galatians 4:4–6. In the midst of his involved discussion of the Law and Christ, Paul writes to the Galatians: "But when the fullness of time had come, God sent forth his Son, born from woman, born under the Law, to redeem those under the Law, so that we might receive adoption as sons" (Gal 4:4–5). The Fathers read this text as summing up Christ's Incarnation and redemptive death. The "sending forth" is the Incarnation of the eternal Son of God, who is truly born a human being "from woman," under the present conditions of our fallen state. The Father sent forth the Son to redeem us and accomplish our adoption as sons. The crucial addition here is the link in the text between the Son *(huios)* who is sent, and the consequence of his sending, our adoption as sons *(huiothesia).* What is the purpose of God's redeeming work in Christ? That we be adopted as sons in the Son. Here we see something further about the enrichment Christ came to bring: He extends to us a share in his own sonship. From here one need travel only a short distance to arrive at Augustine's formulation, "The Son of God became the Son of man that he might make the sons of men the sons of God."[27]

---

[27] For the theme of exchange in Paul, especially in Gal 4, see Morna D. Hooker, "Interchange in Christ," *Journal of Theological Studies,* New Series 22 (1971), 349–61.

Romans 8:14–17, 29. The text on sonship in Romans 8 provides an important link with Galatians 4, and introduces the irreplaceable role of the Holy Spirit in bringing about our sonship in Christ. In these verses, Paul shows the essential connection between the gift of the indwelling Holy Spirit and our sonship in Christ. Those who are led by the Spirit of Christ are "sons *(huioi)* of God" and have within them the Spirit of "sonship/adoption" *(huiothesia).* Because we have received the Spirit of the Son, we are enabled to call on God as our Father, just as the Son does. It is perhaps no accident that within the New Testament, only in these two texts (Rom 8:15 and Gal 4:6) is our sonship linked to the privilege of calling God "Abba." The conclusion to this section (Rom 8:29–30) points to the goal of our sonship in Christ: we are to be "conformed to the image of his Son." God's purpose in sending the Son is that we be made like the Son. This notion is reinforced in 2 Corinthians 3:18, where Paul speaks about our being transformed into his "image" from one degree of glory to another. How, then, has Christ enriched us? By assuming our humanity and redeeming us in and through that humanity, he has given us adoption as sons of God through the Holy Spirit, for the purpose of transforming us to be made progressively into the image of the Son himself.

1 John 3:1–2. These brief verses from the First Letter of John corroborate and expand what we have seen in Paul. John tells us that the Father's love is shown just in this, that we should be called "children of God" *(tekna theou)*—and that is what we really are. The primary goal of the love of God is that we become his children. John then underlines what we are even now—children of God—in order to accentuate what we will become when Christ is fully manifested. While we are not able to see all that we will become (and here John clearly has the resurrection of the body in view), we do know that we shall be "like" him, because we shall behold him as he is. It is not difficult to see how very close John is here to Paul in 2 Corinthians 3:18. It is by beholding the glory of the Lord as he is that we are changed into his very image. We are to be sons and daughters who are like the Son. But here, the fullness of transformation is reserved for the age to come. We are God's children now, but we will (somehow) become "like" the Son in a much more profound way when the Son appears in his glory.

Old and New Adam. If these texts supply the scriptural foundation for the formula of exchange, it is the biblical notion of Christ as the New and Second Adam that provides the wider theological framework. The explicit identification of Christ as the New Adam appears in Romans 5 and 1 Corinthians 15—and these are crucial texts showing Christ as the one who overcomes Adam's sin, and the effect of that sin, namely, death. Jesus Christ, raised from the dead, is now the firstfruits of a new humanity that is cleansed from sin and capable of bearing the life of the Holy Spirit. Paul could not be clearer when he says in 1 Corinthians 15:49: "Just as we have borne the image of the man of dust, we shall also bear the image of the man of heaven." Our redemption is depicted here in terms of the Old and New Adam. Through the redemption accomplished by Christ the New Adam, we are enabled to bear his "image." Though the re-creation of our bodies will happen only at the final resurrection (1 Cor 15:51–52), the transformation of our inner nature into the image of Christ is already underway (2 Cor 4:16).[28]

The biblical term "image" functions as an exegetical link for the Fathers, connecting Adam, the Fall, and the new creation in Christ. Adam, made in the "image and likeness" of God, squandered his inheritance through the primal sin (the precise result of the Fall with respect to our original image and likeness to God is one of the most debated topics in the Christian tradition). And it is only in Christ, the true "image" of God (Col 1:15), that our humanity is restored, filled with the Spirit, and elevated to intimate communion with the Triune God. This is precisely how Irenaeus reads the biblical story of our salvation, interpreting Ephesians 1:10 (the recapitulation of all things in Christ in the fullness of time) explicitly in terms of Christ as the New Adam:

---

[28] The Adam–Christ typology in Paul is the basis for what is often termed the biblical principle of "corporate personality" or "corporate solidarity," in which concrete individuals (Adam and Christ) function also as corporate figures, in whom the whole human race is implicated. For the biblical notion of corporate personality, see Stephen B. Clark, *Redeemer: Understanding the Meaning of the Life, Death, and Resurrection of Jesus Christ* (Ann Arbor: Servant, 1992), 152–60; and J. W. Rogerson, "The Hebrew Conception of Corporate Personality: A Re-Examination," *Journal of Theological Studies,* New Series 21 (1970): 1–16.

> When he became incarnate, and was made man, he recapitulated in himself the long line of human beings, and furnished us, in a brief, comprehensive manner, with salvation; so that what we had lost in Adam—namely, to be according to the image and likeness of God—that we might recover in Christ Jesus.[29] Or how shall man pass into God, unless God has [first] passed into man? And how shall he (man) escape from the generation subject to death, if not by means of a new generation, given in a wonderful and unexpected manner . . . ?
>
> Or how shall they receive adoption from God if they remain in this [kind of] generation, which is naturally possessed by man in this world? . . . But who else is superior to and more eminent than that man who was formed after the likeness of God, except the Son of God, after whose image man was created?[30]

Though other biblical texts could be called upon for support, the key texts on exchange and sonship (2 Cor 8:9, Gal 4:4–6, Rom 8:14–17; 29; 1 Jn 3:1–2), in conjunction with Christ as the New Adam and our transformation into his image (Rom 5:12–21; 1 Cor 15:44–49; 2 Cor 3:18; Eph 1:10) provide the primary biblical foundation and framework for the formula that the Son of God became as we are so that we might become as he is.

We should give brief attention to the unevenness and inequality of this "exchange." To say—as some of the Fathers do—that "we gave him our humanity" contains a double irony. First, it was the Father through the eternal Word who gave us our humanity in the act of creation in the beginning—an act of simple divine gratuity. And the humanity he gave to Adam was pure and undefiled. What *we* gave (back) to the Word was a fallen humanity, disfigured by sin and subject to death. And it is this fallen humanity that he assumed in his divine mercy and condescension. Second, it is quite ironic to say that "we gave him our humanity," as if we were actively offering something to him, however modest the gift. The initiative was entirely on the side of God, who in the fullness of time sent an angel to Mary to announce his purpose to redeem the race. Mary's *fiat* is indeed a crucial and indispensable act in the narrative, but it was wholly God's idea and initiative. The "formula

29 *Adv. Haer.* 3. 18. 1; ANF, vol. 1, 446.
30 Ibid., 4. 33. 4; ANF, vol. 1, 507.

of exchange" must always be understood in this ironical way. The exchange was all in our favor, and due entirely to his initiating grace. "For our sake he made him to be sin who knew no sin, so that in him we might become the righteousness of God" (2 Cor 5:21). As Augustine so succinctly puts it: "He accepted death from what was ours, in order to give us life from what was his."[31]

Redeemed Humanity in Christ

The next task is the rediscovery and expansion of the theological narrative that the formula of exchange encapsulates. The following selection from Cyril of Alexandria's *Commentary on John* provides a densely constructed account of this narrative of salvation in terms of the restoration and deification of our nature through Christ's redeemed humanity:

> It was not otherwise possible for man, being of a nature which perishes, to escape death, unless he recovered that ancient grace, and partook once more of God who holds all things together in being and preserves them in life through the Son in the Spirit. Therefore his only-begotten Word has become a partaker of flesh and blood (Heb 2: 14), that is, he has become man, though being Life by nature, and begotten of the Life that is by nature, that is, of God the Father, so that, having united himself with the flesh which perishes according to the law of its own nature . . . he might restore it to his own life and render it through himself a partaker of God the Father. . . . And he wears our nature, refashioning it to his own life. And he himself is also in us, for we have all become partakers of him, and have him in ourselves through the Spirit. For this reason we have become "partakers of the divine nature" (2 Pet 1: 4), and are reckoned as sons, and so too have in ourselves the Father himself through the Son.[32]

The formula of exchange is firmly embedded within this eloquent statement of our redemption. Because of the desperate plight of the human

---

31 *Serm.* 232. 5; St. Augustine, *Sermons* III/7, trans. Edmund Hill (New Rochelle, NY: New City Press, 1993), 26.

32 *Comm. In Jo.* 14:20; Pusey, vol. 2, 485–86. Unless otherwise noted, translations of Cyril of Alexandria's *Commentary on John* are made by the author and are based on *Sancti patris nostri Cyrilli Archiepiscopi Alexandrini in d. Joannis Evangelium,* 3 vols., ed. P. E. Pusey (Oxford: Clarendon Press, 1872).

race, the one who is Life by nature (the eternal Son of God) fully partook of what was ours (human nature), so that he might grant to our humanity what belongs to him (life), and restore us to participation in God himself. This is a thoroughgoing Trinitarian account of the redemption of our nature in Christ. The Son as the offspring of the Father restores our nature in himself, and we partake of him through the Spirit. Consequently, we are truly "sons of God," "partakers of the divine nature," and sharers in the divine life of the Trinity. A similar account of salvation is expressed at a much later date by John Henry Newman:

> It would seem, moreover, as I have said, that [Christ] has done so by ascending to the Father; that his ascent bodily is his descent spiritually; that his taking our nature up to God, is the descent of God into us; that he has truly, though in an unknown sense, taken us to God, or brought down God to us, according as we view it. Thus, when St. Paul says that our life is hid with Christ in God, we may suppose him to intimate that our principle of existence is no longer a mortal, earthly principle, such as Adam's after his fall, but that we are baptized and hidden anew in God's glory, in that Shekinah of light and purity which we lost when Adam fell—that we are new-created, transformed, spiritualized, glorified in the Divine Nature—that through the participation of Christ, we receive, as through a channel, the true presence of God within and without us, imbuing us with sanctity and immortality.[33]

This perspective is captured poetically in the final (and infrequently sung) verse from Charles Wesley's renowned carol, "Hark the Herald Angels Sing":

> Come, Desire of Nations, Come! Fix in us thy humble home.
> Rise, the woman's conquering seed, bruise in us the serpent's head.
> Adam's likeness now efface; stamp thine image in its place.
> Second Adam from above, reinstate us in thy love.

It is quite evident that the Incarnation of the Son of God, as the New and Second Adam, is in the forefront here. But does this short-

[33] *Lectures on Justification,* 6th ed. (London: Longmans, Green, and Co., 1892), 218–19 (lecture 9).

hand way of summing up our redemption in Christ bypass the hard road of the Cross and the costly redemption from sin that Christ won for us? In the modern period, this very criticism has been leveled at the Fathers—that their presentation of God's work in Christ puts far too much weight solely on the Incarnation (that God became man); that it ignores the sin problem and the work of the Cross; and that it presents a kind of mechanical redemption of our nature simply by virtue of God becoming man. This deficient view, purportedly held by the Fathers, is sometimes called a "physicalist" account of redemption, because of its presumed claim that our nature *(physis)* is redeemed simply by means of the Incarnation alone.

But this is a misrepresentation of what the formula of exchange means.[34] When the Fathers assign critical significance to the Word becoming flesh, they are not delimiting this simply to the conception and birth of Christ, as if the rest of his life were somehow secondary and dispensable. For them, the Incarnation is the inauguration of one united work, which encompasses the whole of Christ's life, passion, death, resurrection, and ascension as Lord to the right hand of the Father. The formula of exchange identifies, as it were, the two poles of our redemption—the critical inauguration of this work in the Incarnation and the final result in our divine filiation—and *assumes* the entire life and work of Christ within the span of these two poles. When we speak of the Incarnation in this sense, then, we are describing the whole work of redemption by its opening act.[35]

---

[34] For a refutation of the view that the Fathers adopted a "physicalist" account of redemption, see J. N. D. Kelly, *Early Christian Doctrines,* rev. ed. (Peabody, MA: Prince Press, 2003), 173–74, 396–99; and Gustaf Aulén, *Christus Victor,* trans. A. G. Herbert (London: SPCK, 1970), 16–35, 81–100.

[35] Two classic treatises on the "Incarnation" confirm this conclusion. Thomas Aquinas's "Treatise on the Incarnation" (*Summa theologiae* III, qq. 1–59) notably includes Christ's death, resurrection, and ascension, and Aquinas concludes the whole treatment with the words, "Let what has been said of the mystery of his Incarnation suffice for the present." Likewise, Athanasius's work, *On the Incarnation,* is ironically far less concerned with the Word becoming flesh, and much more occupied with his saving death on the Cross. For the Incarnation understood in terms of the Passion, and for the Cross being at the center of Athanasius's theology, see John Behr, *The Nicene Faith,* part 1 (Crestwood, NY: St. Vladimir's Press, 2004), 184–207.

Philippians 2:5–11 is decisive here. In this text—the preeminent one in the patristic period for summing up the work of God in Christ—Paul presents the whole sweep of Christ's earthly life—his becoming flesh, his death on the Cross, his resurrection and ascension as Lord—as one united work. When the Fathers speak in shorthand through the formula of exchange, they are only imitating the example of Paul in 2 Corinthians 8:9. They are not bypassing the ministry of Christ, or the preaching of the Gospel, or his sacrifice of atonement for sin, or our reception of redemption through faith and repentance. Rather, they are including the whole of Christ's life when they assert that "the Son of God became the son of man, so that the sons of men might become the sons of God." Eric Mascall underlines this point clearly, stating that there can be no rivalry set up between Christ's Incarnation and his sacrificial death: "There is therefore no question of the Incarnation and the Passion being competitors in the re-creation of man. If it was necessary for manhood to be assumed, it was no less necessary for it to be sacrificed."[36]

There is nonetheless something noteworthy about summing up the work of Christ in terms of the redemption of our nature through Christ as the New and Second Adam. On this view, the Son of God did not merely come on a divine rescue mission, to do a job that no other could do, and then return back again to where he was before. He is not the superhero who appears in the nick of time to rescue us, but who then disappears from view once the job is completed. Rather, the one who redeemed us by his blood is also the New Adam, the new head of a restored human race. Here the atonement accomplished on the Cross is embedded with the Adam–Christ narrative. It is by taking up our humanity and redeeming it in himself that the Son accomplishes our salvation. And the consequence of this is that we are enabled to be joined to him, and through the Spirit to be transformed progressively into his image. Christ himself as the Second Adam becomes the locus of what we are to become as "sons of God."

For this reason, the Fathers tend to interpret all the main events of the life of Christ as contributing to the renewal of our nature in Christ himself. By being born of Mary in our humanity, the Son of God

[36] *Christ, the Christian and the Church,* 76.

assumes our nature in order to effect the restoration of that nature. At his baptism, the incarnate Son receives the Holy Spirit, not only for his own unique mission as Messiah, but also as a representative reception of the Spirit for the human race, providing for the Spirit a fitting temple for his dwelling. By resisting the devil both in the wilderness and in Gethsemane, the New Adam conquers where the Old Adam failed, and by his obedience wins the victory over Satan. By offering himself as the perfect sacrifice for sin, the Son takes our punishment upon himself, cleanses our nature from the stain of Adam's sin, and inaugurates the new humanity. And by his resurrection and ascension, he raises up our nature to new life, and opens up the way for "many sons" (Heb 2:10) to be joined to their heavenly Father (Eph 2:6). John of Damascus neatly describes this theological narrative of Christ as the New Adam, and identifies the complete ministry and work of Christ as contributing to the renovation of our nature:

> Through his birth, that is, his Incarnation, and baptism and passion and resurrection, he delivered our nature from the sin of our first parent and death and corruption, and became the first-fruits of the resurrection, and made himself the way and image and pattern, in order that we, too, following in his footsteps, may become by adoption what he is himself by nature, sons and heirs of God and joint heirs with him. He gave us therefore, as I said, a second birth in order that, just as we who are born of Adam are in his image and are the heirs of the curse and corruption, so also being born of him we may be in his likeness and heirs of his incorruption and blessing and glory.[37]

In the same way Kallistos Ware presents the undivided unity of what he calls Christ's "incarnate dispensation": "The mystery of Christ forms an undivided unity. Incarnation, baptism, transfiguration, crucifixion, resurrection, ascension: all the moments in Christ's incarnate dispensation constitute a single whole. We are saved through the total work of Christ, not just by one particular event in his life."[38]

---

37 *De Fid. Orth.* 4. 13; NPNF, 2nd series, vol. 9, 82. Cf. Gregory of Nyssa, *Cat. Or.* 26.

38 "Salvation in the Orthodox Tradition," 121. Georgios Mantzaridis (*The Deification of Man,* 31), draws the same conclusion: "In other words, the Church Fathers and Palamas are not concerned with the actual moment of the

CHRIST AS BOTH HUMAN AND DIVINE

The presentation of redeemed humanity in Christ would be incomplete and one-sided without due attention to Christ as both human and divine. When Paul contrasts Adam and Christ in 1 Corinthians 15:45, he quotes Genesis 2:7—"The first man Adam became a living being"—and then supplies his own contrasting statement: "the last Adam became a life-giving spirit." Christ, the New Adam, is not simply Adam's worthy replacement—he is much more. He is not just the one who receives the inbreathing of God (Gen 2:7); he is also the one who gives the Spirit. As the Fathers were accustomed to say, he receives the Spirit as man, but he gives the Spirit as God.[39] John the Evangelist expresses this same duality of receiving and giving the Spirit. In the baptism of Jesus, the Spirit descends and remains on him (Jn 1:32–34)—here he is plainly the recipient of the Spirit. But following his resurrection from the dead, Jesus himself, in his resurrected humanity, "breathes" the Spirit on the disciples (Jn 20:22). By this act, Jesus is revealed as the one who renews and fulfills the original inbreathing in Genesis 2:7. He breathes the Spirit on the new humanity that he has inaugurated. Commenting on John 20:22, Cyril of Alexandria writes:

> Therefore, in order that we might learn that it is this one who was the creator of our nature in the beginning, and who sealed us by the Holy Spirit, the Saviour again for us bestows the Spirit through a visible inbreathing on the holy disciples, as on the first-fruits of our renewed nature. . . . And just as then he was formed in the image of his creator, so too now, through participation in the Spirit, he is refashioned to the likeness of his maker.[40]

For the Fathers, the divine-human constitution of Christ was absolutely central to his task of redeeming us and renovating our nature.

---

incarnation so much as with the entire fact of God's dispensation as achieved in the person of Christ, who was born, lived, taught, performed miracles, died, was resurrected and ascended into heaven."

39 For example, when referring to Christ's anointing by the Spirit in his baptism, Cyril of Alexandria says: "He is sanctified therefore as man, but sanctifies as God." St. Cyril of Alexandria, *Commentary on the Gospel of St. Luke,* trans. R. Payne Smith (New York: Studion, 1983), 86.

40 *Comm. In Io.* 20:22; Pusey, vol. 3, 135.

The eloquent testimony from the following selections amply demonstrates how Christ is both the agent and, in a sense, the representative recipient of redemption. Irenaeus shows how the mediator between God and man must be both in one, in order to bring friendship between the two:

> Unless it had been God who had freely given salvation, we could never have possessed it securely. And unless man had been joined to God, he could never have become a partaker of incorruptibility. For it was incumbent upon the Mediator between God and men, by his relationship to both, to bring both to friendship and concord, and present man to God, while he revealed God to man. For, in what way could we be partakers of the adoption of sons, unless we had received from him through the Son that fellowship which refers to himself, unless his Word, having been made flesh, had entered into communion with us? Wherefore also he passed through every stage of life, restoring to all communion with God.[41]

Augustine displays the logic of why our redeemer must be both God and man. For us to be born anew of God, it was fitting that God the Word first be born among men:

> But that men might be born of God, God was first born from among men. For Christ is God, and Christ was born from among men. . . . He was born of God, that we might be made through him; and he was born of a woman, that we might be remade through him. Do not wonder, then, O man, that you are made a son through grace, that you are born of God according to his Word. The Word himself wished first to be born of man, that you might be born safely of God.[42]

And Leo, speaking in the person of Christ, explains the paradox of the twofold nature of Christ for the sake of our salvation:

> I have united you to myself, and I have become the Son of Man, so that you can be the sons of God. Granted that I am one in both,

41 *Adv. Haer.* 3. 18. 7; ANF, vol. 1, 448.

42 *Trac. In Io.* 2. 15; St. Augustine, *Tractates on the Gospel of John 1–10,* trans. John W. Rettig, Fathers of the Church, vol. 78 (Washington, DC: Catholic University of America Press, 1988), 72–73.

> nevertheless, where I am conformed to you, I am less than the Father; but in that I am not divided from the Father, I am also greater than myself. And so, let the nature that is less than the Father go to the Father, and let the flesh be where the Word always is.[43]

We are now in a position to return to the formula of exchange with greater clarity about what this expression means. By asserting that "the Son of God became the Son of Man, so that the sons of men might become the sons of God," the Fathers were attempting to sum up the scriptural testimony concerning our redemption. Christ, by virtue of his divine-human constitution and by means of his saving actions, is the center and locus of that redemption. He is the Second Adam who renews our nature in himself, thus inaugurating a new humanity, and breathes his Spirit into us, causing us to be adopted as sons and daughters of the Father. By means of the indwelling of God, we are set on a course in which we freely cooperate, to be conformed to the image of the Son (Rom 8:29). It is only in the life of the age to come that this transformation will be completed, and we shall see him as he is (1 Jn 3:2). This account of our redemption embraces the full expanse of the biblical narrative, from Adam to Christ, and the glory that awaits us in the new creation. It incorporates the victory of Christ over the enemies and ills that beset the human race: the power of indwelling sin, the slavery of the devil, and the curse of death on our nature. And it is both Christocentric and Trinitarian: The Father sends his Son in our fallen humanity, to redeem the human race and to win for us adoptive sonship through the Spirit.

FROM THE FORMULA OF EXCHANGE TO THE LANGUAGE OF DEIFICATION

At this point the question may be asked, How did we move from this account of the redemption of our nature in Christ to the language of deification? Why was this language employed, and how was it warranted? Certainly some of the foremost proponents of the formula of exchange, such as Irenaeus and Leo, do not use the language of deification, and others, such as Cyril of Alexandria and Augustine, use it

[43] *Serm.* 77. 5 (Freeland, 344, adjusted).

somewhat sparingly. In the concluding chapter the broader warrant for the terminology of deification will be taken up. Here I will limit the discussion to the issue of the origin of the language of deification in the early Church, and how the early use of deification terminology is tightly bound to the redemption of our nature in Christ himself and our adoption as "sons in the Son" through the Spirit. In this context, I will also take up the role played by two biblical texts, Psalm 82:6 and 2 Peter 1:4.

There has been a longstanding judgment that both the language and the concept of deification were foreign intrusions into the Christian faith from the world of Greek philosophy and the mystery religions of the ancient world. Adolph Harnack famously argued that Irenaeus (and those who followed him), by employing the formula of exchange and by depicting salvation as "the deifying of the human race through the incarnation of the Son of God," adopted a view of salvation that derived from the ancient mystery religions. Harnack concludes from this that

> when the Christian religion was represented as the belief in the incarnation of God and as the sure hope of the deification of man, a speculation that had originally never got beyond the fringe of religious knowledge was made the central point of the system and the simple content of the Gospel was obscured.[44]

This is a serious charge, and others continue to revisit this case against the notion of Christian deification.[45]

The early Christians certainly were aware of—and normally quite critical of—the various forms of religious and philosophical currents of their day. Norman Russell concludes his investigation of deification in the Graeco-Roman world with this observation:

---

44 *History of Dogma,* vol. 2, trans. Neil Buchanan (Gloucester, MA: Peter Smith, 1976), 10–11, 317–18.

45 For a more contemporary version of this critique, see Benjamin Drewery, "Deification," in *Christian Spirituality: Essays in Honour of Gordon Rupp,* ed. Peter Brooks (London: SCM Press, 1975), 33–62. He concludes that "the pedigree for 'participation in the divine nature' is to be sought, not in biblical revelation, but in Greek philosophy" (54). It is telling that Drewery, in order to make his case, insists on understanding the patristic doctrine of divinization in ways contrary to the explicitly stated intent of the patristic authors themselves.

> Christians were part of the Graeco-Roman world and interacted with it. They were familiar with the idea of deification from the beginning, not only from the philosophical schools but also from the ruler-cult, the mysteries, and the study circles of popular teachers. Even if they repudiated it, they lived on intimate terms with it.[46]

But Russell and other scholars of the history of deification also argue that the Christian teaching on deification was quite distinct, in both content and vocabulary, from other varieties.[47] It was a counter-proposal to Graeco-Roman views rather than a capitulation to them.[48] Louis Bouyer argues for just this conclusion:

> It must be recognized that the idea of a "divinization" of religious people is purely Christian and has no real antecedent in early Greek writing. . . . But what do these words mean [the technical language of deification] in these writings when they are applied to a faithful Christian? Certainly nothing but the reality of our sharing in the divine sonship recognized as proper to Jesus, the Son of God made man precisely to offer us this possibility.[49]

Though terms for deification first appeared in the pagan Hellenic climate, Christians shied away from using the most characteristic pagan words, and tended to utilize terms that were rare or unknown in the pagan environment to describe Christian realities. This offers some evidence that Christians were conscious of the difference between pagan and Christian conceptions of deification and sought to distinguish them by employing a distinctive vocabulary. In his historical study of the terminology, Russell observes that Christian authors "had to hand a relatively unexploited set of terms with a wide range of meaning which they could adapt to their own purposes without much difficulty," and he concludes that "in the development of the idea of deification and its

---

46 *The Doctrine of Deification,* 50.

47 Ibid., 52; see also Gross, *The Divinization of the Christian,* 2.

48 Balthasar (*Theo-Drama,* vol. 4, 245) concludes that the exchange formula "is not due to some irruption of Greek thought into the biblical milieu: it results from the effort made to secure the full soteriological meaning of the New Testament's *pro nobis.*"

49 *The Christian Mystery,* 227.

distinctive vocabulary, it was Christianity that led the way."[50] The much championed Neoplatonic use of the terminology of divinization in fact chronologically *followed* Christian usage (in Clement and Origen), and may have been dependent upon Christian sources.[51]

On close inspection, one finds that the early Christians who used the terminology of deification, far from being simple enthusiasts for ideas and concepts drawn from Greek thought and religion, were attempting to describe a biblical account of our filiation in Christ through the Holy Spirit. In fact the specifically Jewish context, well chronicled by Gross and Russell, may be even more significant than the Graeco-Roman environment for the emergence of the notion of deification in Christianity.[52] And surprisingly, a short text from the Old Testament, Psalm 82:6, turns out to have been the primary spur and warrant for the development of the technical terminology of deification.

Psalm 82:6. According to the Greek text of this Psalm, the Lord God stands in the assembly "of the gods" and gives judgment against them (v. 1). In vv. 6–7, he addresses his auditors as both "gods" and "sons of the Most High," who will nevertheless die like (mere) men because of their failure to judge in righteousness. The specific warrant for applying the terms "gods" in Psalm 82:6 to human beings is the testimony of Jesus himself in John 10:34–35, where he reasons that if Scripture calls "gods" those to whom the word of God came, then he (Jesus, the one sent directly from the Father) should not be condemned for calling himself "the Son of God." What is critical in both the Psalm and in Jesus' citation of it is the coincidence of the terms "gods" and "sons." It is precisely because of this coincidence that the early Fathers saw in this psalm a shorthand account of our destiny in Christ, and believed themselves warranted to identify as "gods" those who are "the sons of God" through Christ.

---

50 *The Doctrine of Deification,* 52. Note also his conclusion (344): "Christian writers were thus successful in evolving their own distinctive terminology for deification."

51 Ibid., 343. "The Christian usage of deification terms expressing the soul's ascent to God precedes the pagan usage rather than the other way round, as is often assumed" (8).

52 Gross, *The Divinization of the Christian,* 7–79; Russell, *The Doctrine of Deification,* 53–78.

This is just how the second-century Christian apologist Justin Martyr interprets Psalm 82:6 in his *Dialogue with Trypho.* He cites these verses to show that Christians are truly children of God, and he reads the Psalm in its entirety as a prophecy of what is proclaimed in John 1:12–13, that through Christ we have been given the power to become children of God.[53] In the same way, Irenaeus cites Psalm 82 as designating our graced adoptive sonship in Christ:

> And again: "God stood in the congregation of the gods, he judges among the gods." He [here] refers to the Father and the Son, and those who have received the adoption; but these are the Church. For she is the synagogue of God, which God—that is, the Son himself—has gathered by himself. . . . But of what gods [does he speak]? [Of those] to whom he says, "I have said, you are gods, and all sons of the Most High." To those, no doubt, who have received the grace of the "adoption, by which we cry, Abba Father" (Rom 8:15).[54]

Clement of Alexandria, the first Christian author to employ the language of deification, also applies Psalm 82:6 to our baptism into Christ, by which we become "sons" and "gods," and share in his divine life and light:

> The same also takes place in our case, whose exemplar Christ became. Being baptized, we are illuminated; illuminated, we become sons; being made sons, we are made perfect; being made perfect, we are made immortal. "I," says He, "have said that you are gods, and all sons of the Highest." This work is variously called grace, and illumination, and perfection, and washing: washing, by which we cleanse away our sins; grace, by which the penalties accruing to transgressions are remitted; and illumination, by which that holy light of salvation is beheld, that is, by which we see God clearly.[55]

---

[53] *Dial.* 1. 124. For this reading of Justin, see Carl Mosser, "The Earliest Patristic Interpretation of Psalm 82, Jewish Antecedents, and the Origins of Christian Deification," *Journal of Theological Studies,* New Series 56 (2005): 35–41.

[54] *Adv. Haer.* 3. 6. 1; ANF, vol. 1, 419. For other citations of Ps 82:6 in Irenaeus, see *Adv. Haer.* 3. 19. 1; 4. 38. 4.

[55] *Paed.* 1. 6; ANF, vol. 2, 215. For Clement's use of Ps 82:6, see Mosser, "The Earliest Patristic Interpretation of Psalm 82," 54–58.

What conclusions can we draw from these early Christian testimonies to the interpretation of Psalm 82:6? First, the application of Psalm 82:6 to our filial adoption in Christ *predates*—and is also concurrent with—the appearance of the technical terminology of deification in Christian writers. As Carl Mosser concludes, "the patristic citation of Psalm 82:6 was not an ex post facto attempt to provide warrant for alien terminology imported into the Christian tradition by well-meaning Hellenizers."[56] Rather, it was precisely the Christian adaptation of this Psalm, very probably building on an earlier Jewish exegesis, that ushered in the practice of identifying Christians as "gods."[57]

Secondly, the pairing of "gods" and "sons of the Most High" in Psalm 82:6 supplied the early Church with a biblical bridge between our adoptive sonship and our being called "gods" in a clearly defined and delimited way. What does it mean that Christians are called "gods"? It means exactly what the New Testament teaches about our being "sons of God" through Christ and in the Holy Spirit. And how did all this come to pass? "The Son of God became the son of man, in order to enable the sons of men to become sons of God." In a vast majority of cases, the technical terminology of deification in the early Church describes just this: our becoming "sons of God" by grace. The formula of exchange and the language of deification are two ways of expressing the same reality.

2 Peter 1:4. To conclude this discussion on the development of the terminology of deification, some attention must be given to the embattled text of 2 Peter 1:4:

> His divine power has granted to us all things that pertain to life and godliness, through the knowledge of him who called us to his own glory and excellence, by which he has granted to us his precious and very great promises, that through these you may escape from the corruption that is in the world because of passion, and become partakers of the divine nature *(theias koinōnoi physeōs).*

---

56 Ibid., 58.

57 For the Second Temple Jewish antecedents to the interpretation of Ps 82, see Mosser, "The Earliest Patristic Interpretation of Psalm 82," 60–72.

The final phrase is the center of controversy. What does it mean to say that, by God's divine power, we may become "partakers of the divine nature"? Does this text potentially threaten the clear biblical distinction between Creator and creature? Should we, like some contemporary commentators, jettison this text as irredeemably infected with Greek philosophy and so foreign to the true, biblical gospel?[58] Or can we more modestly just ignore this verse as an obscure text that we need not really bother about? Those committed to the Church's biblical canon can hardly accept the first option; those who seek to bring the entire biblical testimony into play will not easily or readily settle for the second.

When we examine how the Fathers do in fact interpret 2 Peter 1:4, we find that in no way do they understand this text as compromising the fundamental distinction between God as Creator and human beings as creatures. Instead, they construe it as stating in bold, demonstrative language just what Paul and John teach concerning our filial adoption as "sons of God." Citations of 2 Peter 1:4 (and of 2 Peter more generally) appear rather late in the Fathers, and even then only at first within the Alexandrian tradition: Origen, Athanasius, and most especially Cyril.[59] Commenting on Romans 5:5, Origen applies 2 Peter 1:4 directly to our becoming "sons of God" by adoption through the gift of the indwelling Holy Spirit, who infuses the love of God into our hearts. This leads in turn to communion with the Father and the Son through the Spirit:

> From the fullness of the Spirit, the fullness of love is infused into the hearts of the saints (Rom 5:5) in order to receive participation in the divine nature, as the apostle Peter has taught (2 Pet 1:4), so

---

58 Drewery, "Deification," 54–55, finds it necessary, in order to distinguish true biblical faith from the doctrine of deification, to repudiate 2 Peter as the pseudonymous work of a second century Hellenic Christian, at odds with true biblical revelation.

59 On Origen as the first Christian writer to cite 2 Pet 1:4, see Russell, *The Doctrine of Deification,* 151, and A. L. Kolp, "Partakers of the Divine Nature: The Use of II Pet 1:4 by Athanasius," *Studia Patristica* 17 (1982): 1018. Four references to 2 Pet 1:4 have been located in Origen's extant corpus. *De Princ.* 4. 4. 4; C. Cels. 7. 65; *Hom. in Lev.* 4. 4; *Comm. Rom.* 4. 9. Citations of 2 Pet 1:4 also appear in the early-fifth-century *Macarian Homilies* (4. 9; 25. 5; 39. 1; 44. 9; 49. 3).

> that through this gift of the Holy Spirit, the word which the Lord said might be fulfilled, "As you, Father, are in me and I in you, may they also be one in us" (Jn 17:21). This is, of course, to be sharers of the divine nature by the fullness of love furnished through the Holy Spirit.[60]

Athanasius interprets 2 Peter 1:4 as Origen did, but expands its use not only to show our participation in God through Christ in the Holy Spirit, but also to demonstrate the full divinity of the Son and the Spirit (and so their ontological distinction from us). Ironically, he cites 2 Peter 1:4 to establish the unbridgeable distinction between God and the created order:

> Further it is through the Spirit that we are all said to be partakers of God. . . . If the Holy Spirit were a creature, we should have no participation of God in him. If indeed we were joined to a creature, we should be strangers to the divine nature inasmuch as we did not partake therein. But, as it is, the fact of our being called partakers of Christ and partakers of God shows that the Unction and Seal that is in us belongs, not to the nature of things originate, but to the nature of the Son, who, through the Spirit who is in him, joins us to the Father. This John tells us, as is said above, when he wrote: "Hereby we know that we abide in God and he in us, because he has given us his Spirit" (1 Jn 4:13). But if, by participation in the Spirit, we are made "sharers in the divine nature" (2 Pet 1:4), we should be mad to say that the Spirit has a created nature and not the nature of God. For it is on this account that those in whom he is are made divine.[61]

In Cyril, 2 Peter 1:4 functions as the key text to describe the result of the Holy Spirit indwelling the faithful in baptism: We become sons by adoption through grace and attain to communion with the Triune God.

---

60 *Comm. Rom.* 4. 9. 12; Origen, *Commentary on the Epistle to the Romans: Books 1–5,* trans. Thomas P. Scheck, Fathers of the Church, vol. 103 (Washington, DC: Catholic University of America Press, 2001), 292–93.

61 *Ep. Ser.* 1. 24. *The Letters of Saint Athanasius concerning the Holy Spirit,* trans. and intro. C. R. B. Shapland (New York: Philosophical Library, 1951), 125–26.

> For believing in the Father, Son, and Holy Spirit, and making this confession before many witnesses, we wash away all the filth of sin, and are enriched by the communication of the Holy Spirit, and made partakers of the divine nature (2 Pet 1:4), and gain the grace of adoption.[62]

Contrary to popular assumptions, 2 Peter 1:4 does not seem to have played a significant role in the development of the terminology of deification, which preceded the appearance of 2 Peter 1:4 in the Fathers. Furthermore, this text is never cited by some who made ample use of the vocabulary of deification (for example, the Cappadocian Fathers—Basil, Gregory of Nazianzus, Gregory of Nyssa—and Pseudo-Dionysius). In the Byzantine tradition between Cyril and Gregory Palamas, 2 Peter 1:4 was referenced only occasionally—it was not a significant text. It was the Hesychast controversy (fourteenth century) and the use of this text by Gregory Palamas that brought it back into more common use again in the Christian East.[63] In the West, Augustine never quotes the exact text of 2 Peter 1:4 when considering human filial adoption and deification, but on several occasions he employs a close paraphrase, "partakers of his divinity."[64] Leo the Great—who never employs the terminology of deification—cites 2 Peter 1:4 in the very same context as we find in the Alexandrian Fathers, namely, as depicting the gift of the Holy Spirit given in baptism, making us to be "sons of God." [65] Consequently, though 2 Peter

---

62 *Comm. in Luc.* 3:21–23; R. Payne Smith, 80.

63 For the absence of 2 Pet 1:4 in the Cappadocians and Pseudo-Dionysius, and the paucity of references to it more generally in the Byzantine tradition before Palamas (cited only twice in Maximus the Confessor and once in Symeon the New Theologian), see Norman Russell, "Partakers of the Divine Nature (2 Pet 1:4) in the Byzantine Tradition," in *Kathegetria: Essays Presented to Joan Hussey*, ed. J. Chrysostomides (Camberley: Porphyrogenitus, 1988), 51–67.

64 *Ennar. in Ps.* 138. 1; NPNF, 1st series, vol. 8, 635: "But that Godhead equal to the Father was made partaker of our mortality, not of his own store, but of ours; that we too might be made partakers of his divinity, not of our store, but of his." For the phrase "partakers of his divinity" in Augustine, see also *Ennar. in Ps.* 52. 5; *De Trin.* 4. 2. 4; *Civ. Dei* 9. 16; 21. 16. Augustine cites 2 Pet 1:4 directly on two occasions (*de Gest. Pel.* 42, 65), to refute the use made of this text by the Pelagians, and quotes the verse without comment in *Speculum* 45.

65 *Serm.* 21. 3; 25. 5.

1:4 is an important biblical affirmation of what deification was understood to mean, the early Church did not build its notion of deification on this text. When the Fathers employ 2 Peter 1:4, they typically apply it to indicate just what the formula of exchange describes: our participation in the divine life through Christ and in the Holy Spirit, by which we become and truly are "sons of God." It provides a shorthand and demonstrative way of stating our filial adoption in Christ through the Spirit. Aquinas is an outstanding witness to this application of 2 Peter 1:4 (and indeed of Ps 82:6) in the later Western tradition. When commenting on John 15:9, "As the Father has loved me, so have I loved you," he offers this striking interpretation:

> For he did not love them to the point of their being gods by nature, nor to the point that they would be united to God so as to form one person with him. But he did love them up to a similar point: he loved them to the extent that they would be gods by their participation in grace—"I say you are gods" (Ps 82:6); "He has granted to us precious and very great promises, that through these you may become partakers of the divine nature" (2 Pet 1:4).[66]

With careful nuance, even John Calvin reads 2 Peter 1:4 as indicating "a kind of deification," descriptive of "a grace the magnitude of which our minds can never fully grasp." This is based upon "the fact that God makes himself ours so that all his possessions become in a sense ours," and all this "so far as our capacity allows."[67]

---

66 *Comm. Jn.* 15:9–13 [1999]; Thomas Aquinas, *Commentary on the Gospel of St. John,* trans. and intro. J. A. Weisheipl and F. R. Larcher, vol. 2 (Petersham, MA: St. Bede's, 1999), 397. For citations of 2 Pet 1:4 in Aquinas related to our filial adoption through grace, see *Summa theologiae* I–II, q. 110, a. 3; I–II, q. 112, a. 1; I–II, q. 114, a. 3; III, q. 62, a. 2; *Comm. Jn.* 10:31–42 [1459–60]; *Comm. Eph.* 3:20 [185]; 4:8 [206].

67 *Calvin's New Testament Commentaries,* vol. 12, trans. W. B. Johnston (Grand Rapids, MI: Eerdmans, 1963), 330–31. Calvin is quite careful to avoid any implication that we become God according to his essence, and he distinguishes this biblical sense of divine participation from anything found in Plato. And as in the Fathers, his statements about the consequences of the grace attested to in 2 Pet 1:4 are surrounded by qualifying expressions such as "in a sense," "in a way," and "so to speak."

CONCLUSION

Our study thus far has attempted to give an account of redeemed humanity in Christ himself through the "graced exchange" at the heart of the Gospel. In this account, the formula of exchange ("the Son of God became the Son of Man so that the sons of men might become sons of God") functions both as the key summation of the doctrine of salvation in the Fathers and as a shorthand statement that sums up the content of the doctrine of deification. By stating the beginning and end of our redemption—the Incarnation of the Son of God, and our destiny as adopted and transformed children of God—the formula implicitly includes the whole economy of salvation from the Father through the Son and in the Spirit. Biblically grounded in key texts that point to our filial adoption in Christ through the Spirit (2 Cor 8:9; Gal 4:4–6; Rom 8:14–17, 29; 1 Jn 3:1–2), this account functions within a wider theological narrative from Adam to Christ that describes the renovation and recreation of our humanity in Christ himself through the Spirit.

I have argued that the terminology of deification is rooted in, and is confirmed by, key biblical texts that are interpreted in the Fathers, and in the subsequent tradition, exactly in accord with the account of our redemption summed up in the formula of exchange. The Fathers began to employ the vocabulary of deification not because of a flirtation with Greek thought and religion, but primarily in the interest of defending and explaining the biblical record against what they perceived to be distortions. It is noteworthy that—upon examination of the key texts—the terminology of deification is typically found in contexts where the Fathers are defending and explaining the full divinity of the Son and the Spirit (and so, the doctrine of the Trinity) and the Incarnation of the Son.

The task that now remains is to expand the formula of exchange, and the narrative of salvation that it sums up, in two directions. First, how is it that the sons and daughters of men become the sons and daughters of God through grace? In other words, how is the new humanity in Christ appropriated to us in the Church? Second, what does it mean to say that we are "transformed into the image of Christ" and that we become "gods, not by nature, but by grace"? What are the consequences of this graced exchange for human life and human nature?

CHAPTER THREE

Receiving the Divine Life

Those who by faith in Christ mount up to sonship with God are baptized, not into one of the things made, but into the Holy Trinity itself, through the Word as mediator. . . . Therefore, we who have received the regeneration by the Spirit through faith, are called and are begotten of God.

—Cyril of Alexandria, *Comm. In Jo.* 1:12–14a

THE DOCTRINE of deification, as we have seen, is centered in Christ himself. It is because of his assumption of our humanity, and his redemption of that same humanity in himself, that we are enabled to participate in his divine life—which is the life of the Trinity. What I want to examine in the next two chapters is how we receive and appropriate the divine life in Christ. This is to ask what Paul means when he says, "so that by his poverty you may become rich" (2 Cor 8:9). How are we enriched by what Christ has done? By what means do "the sons of men become the sons of God"? What does Paul mean when he speaks of us being "transformed into his image" (2 Cor 3:18)? The question can be posed in another form. How is it that we become effectively joined to Christ himself, so that we come to share in his own redeemed and transfigured humanity? To ask this most directly: How do we receive divine life and become deified in Christ?

The shorthand answer often given by the Fathers of the Church is that we can be deified only through God's direct agency, and more specifically, through God himself dwelling actively and effectively within us. The argument they employ—used repeatedly to demonstrate the full divinity of the Son and the Spirit—is that only God can properly sanctify and deify. No creature can accomplish this. It is only through the effective *indwelling* of the Son and the Spirit that human beings are regenerated, sanctified, adopted as children of God, and deified. This is a most crucial point. If we fail to grasp it, we will misunderstand the heart of what deification is.

Deification, however, also requires our full response and cooperation. Moreover, it is a process that continues through the whole of our lives, and reaches completion only with the redemption of our bodies in eternal life with God. Here it can be seen how closely synonymous deification and sanctification are. In certain Fathers, for example in Cyril of Alexandria, "sanctification" and "deification" are nearly identical terms.[1] Deification—like sanctification—can be viewed as occurring in three stages: It begins in us at a particular moment, it grows and progresses through the entirety of our earthly life, and it is completed in the life of the age to come. Though there may be a certain artificiality in this division, it is nonetheless useful for outlining the major aspects of the one, integrated work of our deification. The following selection from Thomas Aquinas, taken from his commentary on John 1:12, neatly displays this threefold aspect. Aquinas is speaking on the topic of divine filiation, that is, how we become "sons in the Son":

> So he says, "he gave them power to become the sons of God" (Jn 1:12). To understand this we should remark that men become sons of God by being made like God. Hence men are sons of God according to a threefold likeness to God. First, by the infusion of grace; hence anyone having sanctifying grace is made a son of God. "You did not receive the spirit of slavery . . . but the spirit of adoption as sons," as said in Romans (8:15). "Because you are sons of God, God sent the Spirit of his Son into your hearts" (Gal 4:6). Secondly, we are like God by the perfection of our actions, because

[1] For sanctification as participation in the divine nature in Cyril, see Walter J. Burghardt, *The Image of God in Man according to Cyril of Alexandria* (Washington, DC: Catholic University Press, 1957), 65–83. Frances Young, *Nicaea to Chalcedon* (London: SCM Press, 1983), 252, states that "sanctification is at the heart of Cyril's soteriology," and that the sanctification by Christ of his own humanity by the coming of the Spirit was "basically Cyril's understanding of θεοποίησις (deification)."

> one who acts justly is a son: "Love your enemies . . . so that you may be the children of your Father" (Mt 5:44). Thirdly, we are made like God by the attainment of glory: the glory of the soul by the light of glory, "When he appears we shall be like him" (1 Jn 3:2); and the glory of the body, "He will reform our lowly body" (Phil 3:21). Of these two it is said in Romans (8:23), "We are waiting for our adoption as sons of God."[2]

For Aquinas, our divine sonship is begun in us through the gift of the indwelling Spirit and the impartation of grace; it progresses as we walk in the new life we have received and become like Christ through imitation; and it is completed in the age to come when we are fully transformed, body and soul.[3]

What occupies us in this chapter is the first stage of deification, that is, how deification is *begun* in us. This is to ask by what means we come to share effectively in God's own divine life. The next chapter will address the second stage, namely, how we progress in the divine life we have received, so that we are, in Paul's phrase, "transformed into his image from one degree of glory to another" (2 Cor 3:18).

The Effective Indwelling of God through Baptism and the Eucharist

If it is the case that deification requires the direct agency of God and is grounded in his effective indwelling in us, this leads to the following question: By what *means* does God come to dwell effectively within us? How does this occur? The consistent position adopted by the Fathers, both East and West, is that God comes to dwell effectively in us especially through baptism and the Eucharist. This sacramental location for the divine indwelling requires explanation and elaboration.

---

2 *Comm. Jn.* 1:12 [150]; Weisheipl, 79.

3 The contemporary Orthodox theologian Christoforos Stavropoulos (*Partakers of the Divine Nature,* 30), confirms the view of Aquinas: "The Theosis of Man, his perfect union with God made possible by grace, will be realized completely in the future age after the resurrection of the dead. However, beginning in this life, this union which divinizes people can be made more and more real. Our corrupt and weakened nature ought to be transformed little by little and adapted to eternal life."

When the Fathers speak of baptism and the Eucharist in combination, they are summing up what are called today the "sacraments of initiation." In the early Church—and still today in the practice of the Eastern churches—baptism in water, the anointing with chrism, and participation in the Eucharist occurred at one time and within one extended liturgy. What the Western Church now calls "confirmation" (and the Eastern Church "chrismation") was typically joined to the baptismal rite, and was not distinguished as a separate event in time. The Orthodox scholar John Zizioulas, pointing to the variety of practices in the early Church concerning the ordering of baptism and confirmation, concludes "that the two rites were united in one synthesis both liturgically and theologically, regardless of the priority of any of the two aspects over the other."[4] And so when the Fathers speak of "baptism" they are normally including the anointing with oil that signifies the gift of the Holy Spirit. Indeed, it is difficult to exaggerate how strongly the Fathers link baptism to the gift of the indwelling Spirit in the believer.[5]

The Fathers give ample testimony to baptism and the gift of the indwelling Spirit as the beginning of our divine filiation and deification. Gregory of Nazianzus, defending the full divinity of the Spirit, asks: "Were the Spirit not to be worshipped, how could he deify me through baptism?"[6] Didymus the Blind likewise inquires: "If by baptism, together with God the Father and his Son, the Holy Spirit brings us back to the first image; if by participation he is the cause of our sonship and our becoming gods; and if no creature possesses the power to adopt and to deify; how is he not true God?"[7] Leo the Great

---

4 *Being as Communion,* 128.

5 The influential ecumenical study *Baptism, Eucharist and Ministry* (Geneva: World Council of Churches, 1982), 4–6, insists on the link between participation in Christ's death and resurrection and receiving the gift of the Spirit, and asserts that baptism signifies and effects both in the believer: "In God's work of salvation, the paschal mystery of Christ's death and resurrection is inseparably linked with the Pentecostal gift of the Holy Spirit. Similarly, participation in Christ's death and resurrection is inseparably linked with the receiving of the Spirit. Baptism in its full meaning signifies and effects both."

6 *Or.* 31. 28, trans. Lionel Wickham, *On God and Christ* (Crestwood, NY: St. Vladimir's Press, 2002), 139.

7 *Trin.* 3. 2; cited in Gross, *The Divinization of the Christian,* 198, adjusted.

exhorts us not to squander our divine sonship and participation in the divine nature gained through baptism:

> Realize, O Christian, your dignity. Once made "a partaker of the divine nature" (2 Pet 1:4), do not return to your former baseness by a life unworthy [of that dignity]. . . . Through the sacrament of baptism you were made "a temple of the Holy Spirit" (1 Cor 6:19). Do not drive away such a dweller by your wicked actions and subject yourself again to servitude under the devil.[8]

In a striking passage, Augustine links deification with our justification, and interprets John 1:12 ("power to become sons of God") with our deification by grace.

> It is evident, then, that he has called men gods, who are deified of his grace, not born of his substance. For he justifies, who is just through his own self, and not another; and he deifies who is God through himself, not by the partaking of another. But he that justifies does himself deify, in that by justifying he makes sons of God. "For he has given them power to become sons of God" (Jn 1:12). If we have been made sons of God, we have also been made gods, but this is the effect of grace adopting, not of nature generating.[9]

Cyril of Alexandria, though not employing the terminology of deification here, shows how through baptism we participate in the life of the Holy Trinity through the mediating power of the Word made flesh, and so become "sons of God":

> Those who by faith in Christ mount up to sonship with God are baptized, not into one of the things made, but into the Holy Trinity itself, through the Word as mediator, conjoining to himself things human through the flesh united to him, and being conjoined by nature to the one who begot him, in that he is by nature God. For so the slave mounted up to sonship, through participation with the true Son, called and, as it were, raised up to the dignity which is in

---

[8] *Serm.* 21. 3; Freeland, 79.

[9] *Ennar. in Ps.* 49. 2; NPNF, 1st series, vol. 8, 178, adjusted.

> the Son by nature. Therefore, we who have received the regeneration by the Spirit through faith, are called and are begotten of God.[10]

And Maximus the Confessor links baptism by water and by fire as dual means by which the Holy Spirit causes us to become "gods by grace":

> The Holy Spirit is active in [baptism by water and by fire]. As water he purifies the defilement of the flesh, and as the Spirit he cleanses the stain of the soul. As the Holy Spirit he establishes as preliminary the way of the virtues, and as fire he make a person God by grace, radiating on him the divine characteristics of virtue.[11]

For the Fathers, as baptism is the occasion of the beginning of our divine filiation and deification, so the Eucharist is the primary means for ongoing participation in the life and power of God. By it we continue to be invigorated by divine life and power. Gregory of Nyssa speaks of deification through the Eucharist in the clearest of terms:

> Since, then, that God-containing flesh partook for its substance and support of this particular nourishment also, and since the God who was manifested infused himself into perishable humanity for this purpose, viz. that by this communion with Deity mankind might at the same time be deified, for this end it is that, by dispensation of his grace, he disseminates himself in every believer through that flesh, whose substance comes from bread and wine, blending himself with the bodies of believers, to secure that, by this union with the immortal, man, too, may be a sharer in incorruption.[12]

John of Damascus describes the body of Christ as "deified" itself, communicating to us in the Eucharist, like a burning coal, the divine fire and life—and all this because of the life-giving power of the Spirit:

---

10 *Comm. In Jo.* 1:12–14a; Pusey, vol. 1, 136.

11 *Quaestiones et Dubia,* 4; Adam G. Cooper, *The Body in St. Maximus the Confessor: Holy Flesh, Wholly Deified* (Oxford: Oxford University Press, 2005), 207.

12 *Cat. Or.* 37; NPNF, 2nd series, vol. 5, 506. John Chrysostom speaks in a similar way about Christ mingling his body with ours so that we may be united to him: *Hom. 1 Tim. 15. 4,* cited in Gross, *The Divinization of the Christian,* 203–4.

> The bread and the wine are not merely figures of the body and blood of Christ (God forbid!) but the deified body of the Lord itself. . . . And let us apply our eyes and lips and brows and partake of the divine coal, in order that the fire of the longing that is in us, with the additional heat derived from the coal may utterly consume our sins and illumine our hearts, and that we may be inflamed and deified by the participation in the divine fire. . . . For the Lord's flesh is life-giving spirit because it was conceived of the life-giving Spirit. For what is born of the Spirit is spirit. But I do not say this to take away the nature of the body, but I wish to make clear its life-giving and divine power.[13]

Thomas Aquinas uses the metaphor of food and drink to speak of our divine inebriation through the Eucharist: "For the food is not changed into the one who eats it, but it turns the one who takes it into itself, as we see in Augustine. . . . And so this is a food capable of making man divine *(divinum)* and inebriating him with divinity *(divinitate inebrians)*."[14] Finally, we find in Cyril of Alexandria an integration of baptism and the Eucharist as the two coordinated means by which Christ through the Holy Spirit dwells effectively within us:

> How might our bodies be members of Christ? We have him in ourselves sensibly and spiritually. For on the one hand, he dwells in our hearts through the Holy Spirit, and on the other we are partakers also of his holy flesh, and we are sanctified in a twofold way. And he dwells in us as life and life-giving, in order that death which had visited our members might be destroyed through him.[15]

But could this emphasis on baptism and the Eucharist be faulted for a kind of ritualism, as if simply by participating in certain formal rites human beings are "automatically" and extrinsically united to

13 *De Fid. Orth.* 4. 13; NPNF, 2nd series, vol. 9, 83–84.

14 *Comm. Jn.* 6:55 [972], Weisheipl, vol. 1, 386..

15 *Comm. In 1 Cor.* 6:15; Pusey, vol. 3, 263–64. For Cyril's coordination of baptism and the Eucharist as the dual means by which the divine life is imparted to us, see Keating, *The Appropriation of Divine Life in Cyril of Alexandria,* 54–104. In the same way Russell, *The Doctrine of Deification,* 185, identifies in Athanasius what he calls "the sacramental character" of deification: What appears to be a "physical redemption" in Athanasius is in fact a summary of the effects of baptism.

Christ and so are somehow deified?[16] Such a conclusion is a misrepresentation of what the Fathers mean when they identify baptism and the Eucharist as the primary occasion and means of our divine filiation. The Fathers are not exhibiting a fascination with ritual or confining the grace of God to sacramental occasions alone; nor do they regard the administration of baptism and the Eucharist as magically or automatically granting deified status. They are, to the contrary, eloquent in speaking about the power of God's divine word to strike the heart and establish the dwelling of God in the soul. Both Augustine and Cyril of Alexandria interpret the feeding of the five thousand in John 6:1–15 in terms of Christ breaking open the Scriptures and nourishing the soul with the Word of God. Identifying the Word of God in Scripture as "heavenly food" and "spiritual bread," Cyril writes: "The saviour, having mixed the New with the Old, by the law and the teaching of the new covenant, nourishes the souls of those who believe in him to life, that is, to eternal life."[17] Didymus the Blind gives voice to this same conviction: "For it is then that they will be 'gods,' when the Word of God has come to dwell in them, as the Saviour says in the Gospel (Jn 10:34–35)."[18] For the Fathers, the proclamation of the Word of God in the Scriptures is also a means by which God comes to dwell in the soul: "Let the word of Christ dwell in you richly" (Col 3:16).[19] They are also insistent that baptism must be accompanied by a living faith. And following Paul (1 Cor 11:29), they warn that if we approach the Eucharist unworthily, we eat and

16 For example, the authors of the "Introduction" to the English translation of Jules Gross, *The Divinization of the Christian according to the Greek Fathers,* say that "the sacramental quality of patristic deification appears to be highly extrinsic" (xii). They misjudge, I believe, what the Fathers are saying, and they also fail to see that what they prize as individual mystical deification in the Fathers is grounded in, and dependent on, sacramental appropriation of divine life.

17 Cyril of Alexandria, *Comm. in Io.* 6:10; Pusey, vol. I, 415, 418. For Augustine, see *Trac. in Io.* 24. 5–6.

18 *In Zach.* 94. 23; trans. Russell, *The Doctrine of Deification,* 157.

19 Gregory Glazov, "Theōsis, Judaism, and Old Testament Anthropology," in *Theōsis: Deification in Christian Theology,* ed. Stephen Finlan and Vladimir Kharlamov (Eugene, OR: Pickwick Publications, 2006), 28, identifies the theme of receiving God's word in the heart as important for the origination of the notion of deification in the Christian tradition.

drink judgment upon ourselves. The important role of faith and love in our deification will be considered in the next chapter. Here it is enough to say that when the Fathers make reference to baptism and the Eucharist in the context of deification, they are assuming the power of God's word and personal appropriation through living faith in the context of the Church.[20]

Yet there is something crucially important about the emphasis they place on baptism and the Eucharist as the locus of our deification. The accent is not on us—on our personal faith or preparation—but on God and what he does. The emphasis is on divine action and agency, because it is the power of God that cleanses us from sin and regenerates us as sons and daughters of God. The sacramental concern for the body is also an important feature of the patristic witness. The immersion of the body in the water of baptism, the anointing of the body with oil, and the feeding of the body with the body and blood of Christ signify the transformation of the whole of human nature, body and soul, and foreshadow the resurrection of the dead.[21] The appeal to the sacraments in the Fathers, then, reflects an emphasis on God and what he does for our sake in the redemption of the whole of our nature. Though our response of free assent and cooperation is essential, the focus is on God. The contemporary Orthodox theologian Georgios Mantzaridis describes this free and personal reception of divine life through the sacraments that is grounded in divine action and power:

> The sacraments of the Church make it possible for man to enter freely and personally into communion with the divinizing grace which the Logos of God bestowed upon human nature in assuming

[20] On the question of whether the sacraments are dispositive or effective causes of grace and the indwelling of the Spirit, see John P. Yocum, "Sacraments in Aquinas," in *Aquinas on Doctrine: A Critical Introduction,* ed. Thomas Weinandy, Daniel Keating, and John Yocum (London: Continuum/T&T Clark, 2004), 169–74. Yocum shows how Aquinas, following the testimony of the Fathers, came to see the sacraments more clearly as effective, instrumental causes of grace.

[21] For the twofold (spiritual and somatic) quality of the sacraments, see Cyril of Alexandria, *Comm. in Jo.* 3:3–6; 6:53, and John of Damascus, *De Fid. Orth.* 4. 13.

> it. Through the sacraments corrupt man, sprung from the corrupt root of Adam, is united with the new root, that is, with Christ, and partakes of incorruptibility and divine life.[22]

THE BIBLICAL TESTIMONY CONCERNING BAPTISM AND THE EUCHARIST

Baptism. By identifying baptism and the Eucharist as the primary means for the effective indwelling of God that brings about our deification, the Fathers believed they were following the teaching of the Scriptures closely. More precisely, the Fathers found in the Scriptures the divinely inspired testimony that both grounded and confirmed the baptismal and Eucharistic practice of the Church. It is worth our attention, then, to examine how the New Testament presents baptism as the occasion for the indwelling of the Holy Spirit, and the Eucharist as participation in the divine life of Christ. My aim here is not to address the entire biblical testimony to baptism and the Eucharist, or to present a full theology of these sacraments, but simply to show how the Scriptures present baptism and the Eucharist as the occasion for bringing about the effective indwelling of God in the believer.

The original link between baptism and the gift of the Spirit appears in the prediction of John the Baptist, that one is coming—greater than himself—who will "baptize you with the Holy Spirit." This testimony, found in all four Evangelists (Mt 3:11; Mk 1:8; Lk 3:16; Jn 1:33), alerts the reader that Jesus is the one who will usher in a baptism, not just for repentance, but for the gift and power of the Holy Spirit. This link is strengthened by the special appearance and descent of the Holy Spirit at Jesus' own baptism, which immediately follows John's prediction in all four Gospels (Mt 3:16; Mk 1:10–11; Lk 3:21–22; Jn 1:32–33). One line of patristic interpretation sees in the descent of the Spirit on Jesus not only a special anointing for his unique messianic role, but also a *representative* anointing of the Spirit on the New and Second Adam (and so on the new humanity he inaugurates), anticipating our own personal reception of the Spirit in our

[22] *The Deification of Man,* 42.

baptism.[23] John's account of Jesus' baptism states that the Spirit descended and *remained* on him (Jn 1:33). The word "remain"—also translated throughout the Fourth Gospel as "abide"—signals for Cyril of Alexandria a new and permanent dwelling of the Spirit in the human race through Christ. Just as the Spirit "remained" on Christ at his baptism, so the Spirit comes to "abide" in us through our baptism into Christ. This is not a temporary or occasional visitation of the Spirit, but his permanent abiding in us for the full spiritualization of our nature.

The Book of Acts presents the Church's reception of the Spirit as a direct parallel to Christ's own reception. Just as Jesus was anointed by the Spirit at the beginning of his ministry, so is the Church anointed at the commencement of her mission in the world. Christ enjoins the disciples to wait in the city until they receive "the promise from on high," paraphrasing and applying the words that John the Baptist used just prior to Jesus' own baptism: "John baptized with water, but before many days you shall be baptized with the Holy Spirit" (Acts 1:5). The outpouring of the Spirit on the day of Pentecost is closely related to the injunction on baptism (Acts 2:38), and this pattern of baptism linked to the gift of the Holy Spirit is followed, with minor variation in order and details, in a series of episodes that mark the entire landscape of Acts (Acts 8:12–17, 9:17–18, 10:47–48, 11:15–16, 19:3–6).[24]

In the Pauline letters, the effects of the indwelling of the Holy Spirit through baptism are more fully displayed. Titus 3:5 presents the regenerating and renewing effects of the Spirit in the context of the "washing" of baptism: "He saved us, not because of deeds done by us in righteousness, but in virtue of his own mercy, by the washing of

---

23 The notion of Jesus' representative reception of the Spirit at his baptism is found especially in Irenaeus and Cyril of Alexandria. See Daniel A. Smith, "Irenaeus and the Baptism of Jesus," *Theological Studies* 58 (1997): 618–42, and Daniel A. Keating, "The Baptism of Jesus in Cyril of Alexandria: The Re-Creation of the Human Race," *Pro Ecclesia* 8 (1999): 201–22.

24 The variations within the Book of Acts concerning the order of baptism and the giving of the Spirit probably gave rise to the variations in practice in the early Church. Acts normally presents the gift of the Spirit (usually through the laying on of hands) as following baptism, but in certain cases the gift of the Spirit precedes baptism (e.g., Acts 9:17–18, 10:47–48).

regeneration and renewal in the Holy Spirit." Significantly, all this results in our becoming "heirs in the hope of eternal life" (Tit 3:7): It is through baptism and the gift of the Spirit that we become "sons" and "heirs" of God.

In two other passages, Paul introduces baptism and then proceeds to depict the results of baptism in terms of our divine filiation through the Spirit. In 1 Corinthians 6:11, he describes the change the Corinthians have experienced through baptism: "But you were washed, you were sanctified, you were justified in the name of the Lord Jesus Christ and in the Spirit of our God." In view of this, he calls them to shun all immorality, especially that which is against the body, giving the reason in v. 19: "Do you not know that your body is a temple of the Holy Spirit within you, which you have from God? You are not your own; you were bought with a price. So glorify God in your body." Clearly for Paul, the Holy Spirit is not simply the external agent of our sanctification and justification, but through baptism the Spirit comes to dwell within us as in a Temple. Later in the same letter (1 Cor 12:13), Paul employs a different metaphor (namely, drinking), in order to point to the reality of the Spirit's indwelling: "For by one Spirit we were all baptized into one body—Jews or Greeks, slaves or free—and all were made to drink of one Spirit."

In Galatians 3:26–27, Paul again identifies baptism as the occasion for becoming "sons of God": "For in Christ Jesus you are all sons of God, through faith. For as many of you as were baptized into Christ have put on Christ." Then in the verses that immediately follow (Gal 4:4–6)—a text we already examined—he takes up the implication of being a son and heir of God, namely, that the Spirit who lives in our hearts causes us to cry out to God as our Father: "And because you are sons, God has sent the Spirit of his Son into our hearts, crying, 'Abba! Father!' " For Paul, our baptism through faith into Christ effects and secures the indwelling of the Holy Spirit (Eph 2:22), and this indwelling in turn provides the ground for his prayer that we may be progressively strengthened "in the inner man" by the Spirit who has come to abide in us (Eph 3:16).

Returning to the Gospel of John, we find in the dialogue with Nicodemus (Jn 3:3–8)—universally recognized as referring to baptism—a description of our new birth from above by "water and the Spirit." The theme of the coming gift of the indwelling Spirit then becomes one of the central themes of the Fourth Gospel. To the woman at the well, Jesus promises that those who come to him will drink from "living water," plainly a reference to the Holy Spirit: "But whoever drinks of the water that I shall give him will never thirst; the water that I shall give him will become in him a spring of water welling up to eternal life" (Jn 4:14). Three chapters later, Jesus extends the same invitation publicly to everyone at the conclusion of the Feast of Tabernacles: "If any one thirst, let him come to me and drink. He who believes in me, as the scripture has said, 'Out of his heart shall flow rivers of living water' " (Jn 7:37–38). The Evangelist tells us that Jesus is speaking here about the Spirit, which those who believed were to receive. And the reason for this: "For the Spirit was not yet [given], because Jesus was not yet glorified" (Jn 7:39).

What is the meaning of John's puzzling explanation for the delay of the giving of the Spirit? Even a cursory reading of the Bible shows that, in one sense, the Spirit plainly was already given before Jesus' glorification. The Spirit had been active in the world, in the people of Israel, and in the life and ministry of Jesus before his glorification. John is evidently speaking of a new kind of presence, a new manner of gift, that can occur only once the glorification of Jesus is complete. And he signals this quite clearly in his account of Christ's death and resurrection. At the point of Jesus' death, he says that Jesus "bowed his head and gave up his spirit" (Jn 19:30). The Greek text is literally, "he gave over the spirit," and most commentators have seen in this phrase a statement not only of Jesus' death, but also of the "breathing out" of the Holy Spirit made possible because of his redemptive death. Again on Easter day, Jesus "breathes" the Spirit on the disciples, calling them to receive the Spirit (Jn 20:22). By means of this action, Jesus is bringing to fulfillment the original "breathing" by God into Adam (Gen 2:7). Christ is the "life-giving Spirit" (1 Cor 15:45) who brings about a new creation of the human race through the gift of the "in-breathed" Holy Spirit.

The Fourth Evangelist does not explain why this new giving of the Spirit is dependent on Jesus' glorification. It most probably has to do, on the one hand, with Jesus being glorified in his resurrected state. By his glorification—his sacrificial death and resurrection—the work of redemption has been completed (Jn 19:29), and the Spirit can now be poured out by the glorified Lord upon his people, who will now be his Spirit-filled presence in the world. But the Fathers also posit another reason: The Spirit could not be given to dwell in us effectively until our own humanity had been redeemed and glorified in Christ himself. By purifying and glorifying our humanity, he made it a fit place for the Spirit to dwell effectively. By giving the Spirit to dwell within us, he joins us to the temple of his own body: "In [Christ] the whole structure is joined together and grows into a holy temple in the Lord; in whom you also are built into it for a dwelling place of God in the Spirit" (Eph 2:21–22). Just as Christ himself is the true temple of God on earth, so we become a holy temple in Christ as we are joined to him in and by the Spirit.[25]

To summarize: The biblical account—attested in many authors and across many texts—correlates baptism, the gift of the Spirit, and our becoming "sons of God" and heirs with Christ. The Scriptures do not depict the Spirit simply as the external divine agent in our regeneration and sanctification; rather, they place the accent on the Spirit as the internal divine agent who comes to dwell and abide effectively within us. When Jesus promises his disciples the coming of "another Counselor," the Spirit of truth, he adds that "he dwells [literally "abides" or "remains"] with you and will be in you" (Jn 14:16–17). He goes on to say that "in that day you will know that I am in the Father, and you in me, and I in you," and that "my Father will love [the one who loves the Son], and we will come to him and make our home with him" (Jn 14:20, 23). The Fathers understood this to refer to the coming of the Spirit at baptism, through which the Trinitarian God begins to dwell effectively in the believer. Commenting on these verses, Cyril of Alexandria writes:

---

25 On Christ as the true and definitive temple of God, and on the centrality of the temple for understanding God's purpose for the human race, see Yves Congar, *The Mystery of the Temple,* trans. Reginald Trevett (Westminster: Newman Press, 1962), and Michael Dauphinais and Matthew Levering, *Holy People, Holy Land: A Theological Introduction to the Bible* (Grand Rapids, MI: Brazos, 2005).

> [Christ] himself is also in us, for we have all become partakers of him, and have him in ourselves through the Spirit. For this reason we have become "partakers of the divine nature" (2 Pet 1: 4), and are reckoned as sons, and so too have in ourselves the Father himself through the Son.[26]

The chief concern of the Fathers, then, is the abiding of the Holy Spirit in the believer and in the Church. Baptism is understood as the inauguration of this indwelling, but the focus is less on the beginning, and more on the permanent abiding of the Spirit as the cause of our full transformation into the image of Christ. This is why the Fathers often interpret New Testament texts on the Spirit as related to baptism, even when the link is not made explicit in the biblical text—not because baptism itself is their primary focus, but because baptism initiates an enduring "reign" of the Holy Spirit in the life of the believer. And it is just this stable indwelling that God intended for us, as the source of our communion with him and the cause of all our fruitfulness.

The Eucharist. For our purposes here, two texts from the biblical testimony to the Eucharist claim our special attention. The first is 1 Corinthians 10:16–17: "The cup of blessing which we bless, is it not a participation in the blood of Christ? The bread which we break, is it not a participation in the body of Christ? Because there is one bread, we who are many are one body, for we all partake of the one bread." The main point to draw from this Pauline text is that in the Eucharist we partake of Christ himself and are joined to him and to one another as "one body," which is the very body of Christ.[27] The language is quite strong and vivid, and the Fathers interpreted this to mean a real partaking of the divine life in Christ and the benefits he has gained for us. John Chrysostom expresses his amazement at the great gift we receive as we partake of this cup of blessing:

> For what he says is this: "This which is in the cup is that which flowed from his side, and of that do we partake." But he called it a

---

26 *Comm. In Jo.* 14:20; Pusey, vol. 2, 485–86.

27 See Stephen B. Clark, *Catholics and the Eucharist* (Ann Arbor, MI: Servant, 2000), 106–12, for commentary on 1 Cor 10 showing that our participation is in the sacrifice of Christ on the Cross and the benefits he won for us.

> cup of blessing, because holding it in our hands, we so exalt him in our hymn, wondering, astonished at his unspeakable gift, blessing him, among other things, for the pouring out of this self-same draught that we might not abide in error: and not only for the pouring it out, but also for the imparting of it to us all.[28]

The second text is the Bread of Life discourse in John 6. The central frame of this long discourse is Christ himself as the bread of life come from heaven for the life of the world, of which the manna in the desert was simply a type and foreshadowing (vv. 25–40). The last part of the discourse (vv. 51–59), however, unmistakably refers to the Eucharist. Jesus makes a simple identity between himself and "the bread of God" come down from heaven: "I am the bread of life" (vv. 35, 48). Then in v. 51 he specifically identifies the bread with his flesh: "the bread which I shall give for the life of the world is my flesh." In a further claim that gives great scandal, he states that his flesh and blood are to be ingested by the believer for eternal life:

> Truly, truly, I say to you, unless you eat the flesh of the Son of man and drink his blood, you have no life in you; he who eats my flesh and drinks my blood has eternal life, and I will raise him up at the last day. For my flesh is food indeed, and my blood is drink indeed. He who eats my flesh and drinks my blood abides in me, and I in him. As the living Father sent me, and I live because of the Father, so he who eats me will live because of me (vv. 53–57).

The word "abide" in v. 56 is theologically significant. Just as God's Spirit comes to abide in us through baptism (and through the Spirit, the Father and the Son also—Jn 14:20, 23), so by partaking worthily of Christ's body and blood in the Eucharist we receive eternal life and come to "abide" in him. And this abiding is a participation in the *life* of the Father and the Son, as v. 57 makes clear. Commenting on this verse, Augustine says: "Therefore we, eating him, live because of him, that is, by receiving him as eternal life which we did not have from ourselves."[29]

---

28 *Hom. in 1 Cor.* (*Hom.* 24 on 1 Cor 10:16); NPNF, 1st series, vol. 12, 139, adjusted.

29 *Trac. Io.* 26. 19; Rettig, vol. 79, 275.

Cyril glories in the divine life that comes through a living participation of Christ through the Eucharist:

> For since the life-giving Word of God was living in the flesh, he transformed it to his own proper good, that is to life, and according to the manner of the inexpressible union, suitably rendered it wholly life-giving, as he is himself by nature. For this reason the body of Christ gives life to those who partake of it. . . . And since the flesh of the savior has become life-giving (as being united to that which is by nature life, the Word of God), when we taste it, then we have life in ourselves, we too united to it as it to the indwelling Word.[30]

This brief inspection of the biblical testimony enables us to see, at least in part, why the Fathers interpreted the Scriptures as teaching that baptism and the Eucharist are the primary means whereby God himself comes to dwell effectively in us. By the Spirit in baptism and through the life-giving body and blood of Christ through the Eucharist, we have divine life and power dwelling within us—and it is this divine indwelling that is the proper source of our deification.[31]

THE HOLY SPIRIT IN THE WESTERN TRADITION

One goal of this study is to show that the doctrine of deification is found at the patristic root of both the Eastern and Western theological traditions. If the account offered here accurately describes the Eastern tradition, can it really be said to represent the Western tradition as well? Particularly with regard to the indwelling Holy Spirit as the principle of our deification, there is a common view that the Western Church is simply deficient. The account goes something like this: Somewhere between Augustine and Anselm the West lost track of the Holy Spirit as a divine person, active in his own right in the sanctification of the believer and the Church, and it has never fully recovered. As

30 *Comm. In Io.* 6:51; Pusey, vol. 1, 410; *In Io.* 6:53; 418.

31 Stavropoulos, *Partakers of the Divine Nature,* 37–38, writes: "The Holy Mysteries (sacraments) are what transmit this grace of the All-Holy Spirit. His sanctifying and deifying energy is actualized in the holy services of the Church, especially in holy Baptism, Repentance and the Divine Eucharist."

a result, the Western theological tradition has a deficient pneumatology—that is, a deficient account of Holy Spirit and his work in the divine economy of salvation.[32]

It is beyond the scope of this study to address this issue with any comprehensiveness, and some aspects of the criticism—at least for certain periods in Western theology—have merit.[33] It should be readily acknowledged that the Eastern tradition (inclusive of Maximus, Symeon the New Theologian, Gregory Palamas, and Nicholas Cabasilas) has a rich and highly developed account of the specific activity of the Holy Spirit in the sanctification of the Church and the deification of the believer. But I want to show that major representatives and carriers of the Western tradition (namely Ambrose, Augustine, Leo, and Thomas Aquinas) exemplify just the kind of emphasis on the indwelling of the Holy Spirit through baptism, leading to our deification, that I have sketched above.

In defense of the divinity of the Holy Spirit, Ambrose offers a striking testimony to the Spirit as the seal of our adoptive sonship in Christ. Speaking about the Spirit's role specifically in baptism, he declares that it is the Spirit who causes us to be remade in the image of God and who makes us partakers of the divine nature (2 Pet 1:4).

> We were then sealed with the Spirit by God. For as we die in Christ, in order to be born again, so, too, we are sealed with the Spirit, that we may possess his brightness and image and grace, which is undoubtedly our spiritual seal. For although we were visibly sealed in our bodies, we are in truth sealed in our hearts, that the Holy Spirit may portray in us the likeness of the heavenly image. Who, then, can dare to say that the Holy Spirit is separated

32 Vladimir Lossky (*In the Image and Likeness of God,* 103) is the most outspoken proponent of this view. John Zizioulas (*Being As Communion,* 125–41) offers a more balanced critique than Lossky of Western pneumatology, and he also finds fault with various Eastern accounts as well. Other critics of Western pneumatology include Thomas Marsh, *The Triune God* (Dublin: Columba, 1994), 136, 152, and Alasdair Heron, *The Holy Spirit: The Holy Spirit in the Bible, in the History of Christian Thought and in Recent Theology* (London: Marshall, Morgan and Scott, 1983), 94–97.

33 For a presentation of more recent deficiencies in Western pneumatology, see Yves Congar, *I Believe in the Holy Spirit,* trans. David Smith (New York: Crossroad, 1997), 159–64.

> from the Father and the Son, since through him we attain to the image and likeness of God, and through him, as the Apostle Peter says, are "partakers of the divine nature" (2 Pet 1:4)?[34]

For Augustine, the love of God, and our participation in that love, is at the center of things. He repeatedly returns to Romans 5:5: "God's love has been poured into our hearts through the Holy Spirit which has been given to us." Thus, the effective indwelling of the Spirit is central to the whole of the Christian life. As he says in his commentary on John 14:16 (the promise of "another Counselor"): "Let it be established that without the Holy Spirit we cannot love Christ and keep his commandments, and that we can and do do that so much the less as we receive him less, but so much the more as we receive him more."[35] For Augustine, without the effective abiding presence of the Holy Spirit, we cannot even begin to follow Christ's example: "[He promised] that they too should become his witnesses, with the Holy Spirit, of course, working this in them. . . . For indeed, it would have been insufficient to encourage them by his own example, if he were not to fill [them] with his Spirit."[36] Even our participation in the Eucharist, for Augustine, effects participation in the Spirit, such "that we not only eat the flesh of Christ and the blood of Christ in the sacrament as many evil men also do, but that we eat and drink for participation in the Spirit, that we may abide as members in the body of the Lord, that we may be enlivened by his Spirit."[37]

We find a similar testimony to the central role of the indwelling Spirit in the writings of Leo the Great. For Leo, the Spirit is both the divine agent who effects our rebirth in baptism and the divine indweller who comes to live in the soul of the believer as the agent of ongoing sanctification:

> Consider, dearly beloved, and pay careful attention by the light of the Holy Spirit as to who it is who has taken us to himself and

[34] *De Spir.* I. 6. 79–80; NPNF, 2nd series, vol. 10, 103.

[35] *Trac. in Io.* 74. 2; St. Augustine, *Tractates on the Gospel of John 55–111,* trans. John W. Rettig, Fathers of the Church, vol. 90 (Washington, DC: Catholic University of America Press, 1994), 90.

[36] *Trac. in Io.* 93. 1; Rettig, vol. 90, 173.

[37] *Trac. in Io.* 27. 11; Rettig, vol. 79, 286, adjusted.

> whom we have received in ourselves. As the Lord Jesus was made our flesh by being born, so we are made his body by being reborn. Consequently, we are members of Christ and a temple of the Spirit of God (1 Cor 6:15, 19). It is for this reason that the blessed Apostle says, "Glorify God and bear him in your body" (1 Cor 6:20).[38]

Turning to Thomas Aquinas, we find the same understanding: through baptism and the gift of the indwelling Spirit, the whole life of grace unfolds. He presents not a generic notion of grace granted to the believer, but rather the person of the Holy Spirit inhabiting the soul as the source of all life and grace. This selection, coming from his commentary on the woman at the well in John 4, displays with great clarity that the indwelling of the Spirit is the living and personal source of all grace:

> But living water is connected with its source and flows from it. So according to this understanding, the grace of the Holy Spirit is correctly called living water, because the grace of the Holy Spirit is given to man in such a way that the source itself of the grace is also given, that is, the Holy Spirit. Indeed, grace is given by the Holy Spirit: "The love of God is poured out into our hearts by the Holy Spirit, who has been given to us" (Rom 5:5). For the Holy Spirit is the unfailing fountain from whom all gifts of grace flow (1 Cor 12:11). And so if anyone has a gift of the Holy Spirit without having the Spirit, the water is not united with its source, and so is not living but dead (Jas 2:20).[39]

A final selection from John Henry Newman, who speaks in eloquent terms of the accomplishments of the indwelling Spirit, shows that this understanding of the centrality of the Holy Spirit is alive and well in later Western writers. Newman presents the inhabitation of the Spirit,

---

38 *Serm.* 23. 5; Freeland, 91. On the Holy Spirit and our sanctification in Leo, see *Ep.* 15. 9; 31. 3; 159. 7; *Serm.* 21. 3; 24. 3; 25. 5; 27. 6; 29. 1; 35. 2; 38. 3–4; 41. 1, 3; 42. 6; 45. 1; 50. 2; 57. 5; 66. 2, 4; 69. 5; 75. 5; 78. 3; 79. 3.

39 *In. Io.* 4:10–26 [577]; Weisheipl, 239. Servais Pinckaers, *The Sources of Christian Ethics,* trans. Sr. Mary Thomas Noble (Edinburgh: T&T Clark, 1995), 120, writes: "A moral system cannot therefore be called fully Christian . . . unless it gives a preponderant place to the action of the Holy Spirit. This was fully understood later by St. Augustine and St. Thomas."

given through baptism, as the basis for all that Christ came to bring, including our "participation in the divine nature" (2 Pet 1:4):

> It is plain that such an inhabitation [by the Spirit] brings the Christian into a state altogether new and marvelous, far above the possession of mere gifts, exalts him inconceivably in the scale of beings, and gives him a place and an office which he had not before. In St. Peter's forcible language, he becomes "partaker of the Divine Nature" (2 Pet 1:4), and has "power" or authority, as St. John says, "to become the son of God" (Jn 1:12). Or, to use the words of St. Paul, "he is a new creation; old things are passed away, behold all things are become new" (2 Cor 5:17). His rank is new, his parentage and service new. He is "of God" (1 Jn 4:4), and "is not his own" (1 Cor 6:19), "a vessel unto honour, sanctified and meet for the Master's use, and prepared unto every good work" (2 Tim 2:21). This wonderful change from darkness to light, through the entrance of the Spirit into the soul, is called Regeneration, or the New Birth; a blessing which, before Christ's coming, not even the Prophets and righteous men possessed, but which is now conveyed to all men freely through the Sacrament of Baptism.[40]

Conclusion

I have sought to describe the beginning of deification in the human race, that is, how we come to receive, and participate in, God's own divine life. The foundational premise, drawn from a wide testimony of the Fathers, is that human beings can be deified only through God's direct agency, only through having God himself dwelling effectively within them. The primary means for this divine indwelling are baptism and the Eucharist. In baptism we are cleansed from sin, regenerated as children of God, and indwelt by the Holy Spirit. As the Fathers make clear, baptism is the proper beginning of deification in us. In the Eucharist, our communion with the life-giving body and blood of Christ deepens our share in the divine life, and a way is provided for an ongoing participation in Christ's own divine life and power for our progress in deification.

---

[40] "The Indwelling Spirit," in *Parochial and Plain Sermons,* vol. 2. 19 (San Francisco, CA: Ignatius Press, 1987), 366.

The Fathers understood the sacraments of initiation as the primary means—divinely given—whereby we come to share in the blessings of the New Covenant. All that Christ came to accomplish is effected in us by the Spirit of Christ who comes to dwell in us as in a temple—and baptism and the Eucharist are the primary means by which this effective divine indwelling occurs. It is striking that in both the East and the West the primary fruit of the New Covenant in Christ is often summed up in terms of the indwelling of the Holy Spirit. Thomas Aquinas summarizes the "New Law" (by which he means the New Covenant) as consisting chiefly in "the grace of the Holy Spirit."[41] St. Seraphim of Sarov describes the aim of the Christian life as "the acquisition of the Holy Spirit of God."[42] Our deification, then, is dependent on God himself dwelling effectively in us—and this is just what Christ's redeeming work was intended to accomplish. The doctrine of deification is centered on the primacy of divine action. It is a God-centered doctrine.

The divine life is received in such a way, however, as to display the personal quality of our deification in Christ. Our own deification is not the automatic consequence of Christ assuming and redeeming our nature in himself, as if we were somehow "reformatted" impersonally to a deified condition. David Bentley Hart writes: "Human 'nature' is not a concrete universal that, simply through the metabolism of the incarnation, is divinized."[43] Rather, each of us personally receives the Holy Spirit, and each of us personally communes with the life-giving body and blood of Christ. In Ephesians 3:16–17, Paul prays that we may be strengthened with power "in the inner man" through the Spirit, and that Christ "may dwell in our hearts through faith"—this is the language of the personal indwelling of the Spirit and the Son in

41 *Summa theologiae* I–II, q. 106, a. 1–3 (all translations of the *Summa theologiae* are from the translation of the Fathers of the English Dominican Province, 1920); *Comm. in Heb.* 8:10 [404]. For the Holy Spirit as the principle of the New Law in Aquinas, see Matthew Levering, *Christ's Fulfillment of Torah and Temple: Salvation according to Thomas Aquinas* (Notre Dame, IN: University of Notre Dame Press, 2002), 76, 113.

42 Cited in Timothy (Kallistos) Ware, *The Orthodox Church* (London: Penguin, 1964), 235.

43 *The Beauty of the Infinite: The Aesthetics of Christian Truth* (Grand Rapids, MI: Eerdmans, 2003), 326.

the believer. Through Christ and in the Spirit, the divine life comes to us personally, and we must personally receive and appropriate—in the context of the corporate life of the Church—the God who always comes to us personally.

One further implication of the sacramental location of deification, brought out here by Kallistos Ware, is worthy of note: "Deification is not something reserved for a few select initiates, but something intended for all alike. . . . Certainly we shall only be fully deified at the Last Day; but for each of us the process of divinization must begin here and now in this present life."[44] The testimony of the tradition is clear that deification is begun in each of us through our common baptism—at the beginning of our life in Christ. Consequently, deification is not just the crowning endpoint of all that the Father intends for us in Christ through the Spirit; it is also the *beginning* of the work of God in us, and the foundation for our progress in the Christian life.

> Christian theologians, from the Fathers to the present day . . . have been equally convinced that no term less than "deification" is adequate to describe the condition of the human being who has been taken by grace into the supernatural realm; and, let us note, not simply the condition of the mystic united to God in the spiritual marriage or of the saint enjoying the beatific vision in heaven, but also that of the newly baptized infant at the font or of the newly absolved sinner in the confessional.[45]

All Christians, by virtue of their new birth in the Spirit as children of God, are "deified," just as they are all sanctified. As noted earlier, the two terms, deification and sanctification, are nearly synonymous in this context. Just as sanctification in one sense is accomplished in us by God in our conversion and baptism, and yet progresses in us throughout this life and achieves its completion when we are glorified in body and soul in the life of the age to come, so it is with deification. What has been begun in us is intended to progress and grow, in order to reach its completion in the life of heaven.

---

44 *The Orthodox Church* (London: Penguin, 1963), 240.

45 Eric Mascall, *The Importance of Being Human: Some Aspects of the Christian Doctrine of Man* (London: Oxford University Press, 1959), 64.

CHAPTER FOUR

Transformed into His Image

Indeed the Savior's grace re-fashions us to [the image of God] on a daily basis. What fell in the First Adam has been raised up in the Second. But our being re-fashioned has no other cause than the mercy of God. We would not love him but for the fact that "he has loved us first" (1 Jn 4:10), and has dispelled the darkness of our ignorance with the light of his truth.

—Leo the Great, *Serm.* 12. 1

THE TOPIC of human progress in deification is vast, encompassing far more terrain than a summary study of deification such as this could possibly cover. Under the heading "progress in deification" one could include topics such as holiness, freedom, prayer, the theological virtues (faith, hope, and love), the fruit of the Holy Spirit, and more broadly all that concerns our communion with God and our ethical responsibility as disciples of Christ in the world. While acknowledging that all these subjects (and more) pertain to our growth in deification, I will focus more narrowly on three foundational truths concerning our progress in the divine life granted to us through Christ in the Spirit. First, all progress in deification—in its various manifestations—is grounded in divine grace and the prior indwelling of God. Second, the New Testament presents us with—and beckons us to—transformation into full maturity in the image of Christ, expressed especially by faith, hope, and love. Third, our progress in deification has a baptismal and Eucharistic shape. We are called to share progressively in the communion of Christ's suffering, death, and resurrection. These aspects of our deification have been selected because they help us to see the continuity in our path to deification from its beginnings to maturity in this life.

THE PRIORITY OF GRACE AND DIVINE INDWELLING

The priority of divine grace through the indwelling of the Holy Spirit has already been noted in figures such as Augustine and Aquinas, but it warrants some development here as the central principle for all that we can say about progress in deification. To state the matter directly (and paradoxically), it is only because God has declared us and made us to be sons and daughters of God that we are able to make progress in becoming sons and daughters of God. It is only because he has cleansed us from sin, regenerated us, and filled us with his Spirit that we can be transformed into the Son, who is the image of the Father. Leo the Great describes the daily re-fashioning of the image of God in us by the grace of Christ at work within us:

> Indeed the Savior's grace re-fashions us to [the image of God] on a daily basis. What fell in the first Adam has been raised up in the second. But our being re-fashioned has no other cause than the mercy of God. We would not love him but for the fact that "he has loved us first" (1 Jn 4:10) and has dispelled the darkness of our ignorance with the light of his truth.[1]

Our abiding in God and growing into the image of God—our imitation of Christ—depends upon God first coming to dwell effectively in us. In the words of Hans Urs von Balthasar:

> For all is *grace*: being called, being addressed by the Gospel, coming to faith and entering upon the goods of faith through the baptism that confers stability and through the ever greater stabilizing of the Christian life. . . . The language about "remaining" and correspondingly about "indwelling," is reversed: the believer remains and dwells in Christ and in God only because Christ and God dwell in him and remain in him.[2]

The priority of divine indwelling is marvelously expressed by Cyril of Alexandria as he attempts to explain the jarring words of Jesus in John 16:7, "It is to your advantage that I go away":

---

1 *Serm.* 12. 1; Freeland, 49–50.

2 *The Glory of the Lord: A Theological Aesthetics,* vol. 7, trans. Brian McNeil (T&T Clark: Edinburgh, 1989), 308–9.

> How was it not necessary that [Christ] be together with his worshippers through the Spirit, and dwell in our hearts through faith (Eph 3:17), in order that, having him in ourselves, we might cry with boldness, "Abba, Father," and might readily advance in all virtue, and besides this might be found powerful and invincible against the cunning of the devil, and the assaults of men, seeing that we have the all-powerful Spirit?[3]

The Macarian Homilies witness to our need to rely all the more on God's grace as we experience making progress in the divine life of Christ.

> Being completely attached to the cross of Christ, [persons who love God] daily perceive in themselves that they are spiritually progressing towards their spiritual Bridegroom. Having been wounded by the desire for heaven, and thirsting for the justice of the virtues, they await the illumination of the Spirit with the greatest insatiable longing. And should they be considered worthy to receive through their faith knowledge of divine mysteries, or to be made participators of the happiness of heavenly grace, they still do not put their trust in themselves. . . . The more they perceive themselves advancing in spiritual perfection, the more do they hunger and thirst for a greater share of and increase in grace.[4]

The priority of grace—and specifically of Christ's work and our share in that work through the Spirit—is reflected in how the early Church went about the task of biblical exegesis. In his intensive study of patristic and medieval exegesis, Henri de Lubac identifies two distinct models for how the Scriptures were interpreted spiritually in the early Church. In the first (the minority model), the moral or tropological reading (how we are to live) comes before the allegorical or Christological sense (who Christ is and what he has done for us). In the second (the dominant model), the moral reading always follows the Christological. De Lubac argues that the difference between these two models is theologically significant. The second model rightly interprets the divine economy of salvation, because it positions how we are to live on the basis of what God has already done in Christ.

---

3 *Comm. In Jo.* 16. 7; Pusey, vol. 2, 620.

4 *Mac. Hom.* 10. 1; *Pseudo-Macarius: The Fifty Spiritual Homilies,* 88.

> Only the second of the two orders, the one that puts allegory right after history, expresses the authentic doctrine in both its fullness and its purity. It alone gives an adequate rendition of the Christian mystery. . . . When tropology came after allegory—and even sometimes after anagogy—it was sacred. It depended on faith. When it came before, it was profane—in principle, at least.[5]

If we are to interpret the Scriptures theologically, according to the Trinitarian pattern of salvation and the centrality of Christ, all that pertains to our progress must derive from Christ and what he has done for us through the Spirit in the Church.

Servais Pinckaers offers a similar insight into the theological ordering of Aquinas's treatment of the moral life. He observes that the massive study of the virtues in the second part of the *Summa theologiae* is preceded and governed by a treatment of the Trinity, the life of grace, and the infused supernatural virtues:

> In the *Summa theologiae*, St. Thomas always took God, and the things of God, as his starting point, since God was the principle and source of all things in the order of being and truth. . . . In his study of virtues, for example, he began with the supernatural virtues, and first with faith. . . . This was the theological order demanded even of divine science, conveyed through revelation and addressed to faith.[6]

Whether in biblical exegesis or in systematic theology, the divine saving initiative of the Father through the Son and in the Spirit governs—and acts as the wellspring for—all that we can say about our progress in deification.

In this context, the knotty issue of human freedom and cooperation with divine action inevitably arises. Differences and disagreements

[5] *Medieval Exegesis,* vol. 1, *The Four Senses of Scripture,* trans. Marc Sebanc (Grand Rapids, MI: Eerdmans, 1998), 114–15, 137. For the wider treatment of the two models, see 75–159.

[6] *The Sources of Christian Ethics,* 292. Some have found fault with Aquinas for placing his treatment of Christology per se after his treatment of the virtues, but he plainly treats the moral life of the Christian entirely within the New Covenant context of the life of grace and the gift of the indwelling Spirit. For Aquinas's account of the virtues in the *Summa,* see Levering, *Christ's Fulfillment of Torah and Temple,* 108–9.

on this topic are often clouded by a lack of clarity about precisely what is meant by free choice and human freedom. While disagreements may remain, arising especially from the controversies at the time of the Reformation, there are several (often paradoxical) truths upheld by the wider Christian tradition that can shape and guide our thinking on the role of human freedom and cooperation in the work of God. The first has just been outlined: The initiative always lies with God. Human salvation was God's idea and was accomplished by Christ as a free gift of grace. Our ability to respond to the gracious work of God is itself "graced." Grace always comes before and initiates every human response to the offer of salvation in Christ—it is "prevenient." Consequently, there is no room for human boasting: "What do you have that you did not receive? And if you received it, why do you boast as if it were not a gift?" (1 Cor 4:7). In a passage that could have come from the pen of Augustine, Cyril of Alexandria writes:

> For he teaches us, that we must think humbly of ourselves, as being nothing, both as regards human nature and the readiness of the mind to fall away into sin, and as strengthened and being what we are only through him and of him. If therefore it is from him that we borrow both our salvation, and our seeming to be something in virtue and piety, what reason have we for proud thoughts? For all we have is from him, and of ourselves we have nothing. . . . Let us then glory not in ourselves, but rather in his gifts.[7]

A second, coordinate truth is that the attribute of human freedom, of being able to know and freely choose for God and the good, is itself an essential part of the image of God in man. This view is especially pronounced in the Greek patristic tradition, though witnesses in the Latin tradition are not lacking. Basil the Great attributes freedom of the soul to the fact that it was made in the image of God from the beginning: "For it was set free of all compulsion and received from the Creator a life of free choice, because it was made to God's image."[8] Didymus the Blind tells us that after baptism we become what we were

---

[7] *Comm. In Luc.* 22:31–34; Smith, 575–76.

[8] *Quod Deus non est auctor malorum,* 6; trans. Burghardt, *The Image of God in Man,* 43.

originally in Adam, "sinless and free; for these are what the image and likeness signifies."[9] As a representative of the West, Tertullian (early third century) defends the gift of human freedom as being the most noble part of the image and likeness of God: "I find, then, that man was by God constituted free, master of his own will and power; indicating the presence of God's image and likeness in him by nothing so well as by this constitution of his nature."[10]

The pivotal theological issue, however, concerns the status of human freedom after the Fall. Is the human creature after the Fall still free, and if so, to what extent can and does this freedom interact and cooperate with the grace offered in Christ? The Christian tradition broadly answers this question by acknowledging that some significant measure of free choice, given in creation, remains after the Fall, but that full freedom to love God and be in communion with him requires the grace of God to operate in us. Thomas Aquinas writes:

> But if we speak of grace as it signifies a help from God to move us to good, no preparation is required on man's part, that, as it were, anticipates the Divine help, but rather, every preparation in man must be by the help of God moving the soul to good. And thus even the good movement of the free-will, whereby anyone is prepared for receiving the gift of grace is an act of the free-will moved by God.[11]

This is the third truth: True freedom to love God, to do his will, and to be in full communion with him is regained for the human race only in Christ, the New Adam. In his study of the moral life, Pinckaers writes:

> The nearer man approaches to God through the moral progress that weakens his inclination to sin, the more he grows in full freedom, sharing in the divine freedom itself. The blessed have therefore lost none of their freedom; rather, they have become supremely free as God is free, through the grace of Christ and the work of the Holy Spirit.[12]

---

9 *De Trin.* 2. 12; trans. Burghardt, *The Image of God in Man,* 44. See Burghardt, 40–50, for a survey of patristic teaching on freedom as part of the image and likeness of God in the human race.

10 *Adv. Marc.* 2. 5; ANF, vol. 3, 301. See also *Adv. Marc.* 2. 6, 9.

11 *Summa theologiae* I–II, q. 112, a. 2.

12 *The Sources of Christian Ethics,* 376.

What then can we say about human cooperation with the grace of God in Christ? The broad testimony of the Christian tradition, East and West, is not that God bypasses us in saving us, but that by his grace he enables us to respond and cooperate freely with his free gift of salvation. We are not free *in and from ourselves* to respond and cooperate with the work of salvation, but by his graced action in us, God enables us to respond and cooperate with genuine freedom. Leo the Great is a witness to human cooperation with the grace of God, basing his interpretation on a reading on Philippians 2:12–13:

> If we are of one mind with him (willing what he wills, disapproving of what he disapproves), he himself will bring us to victory in all our battles. He who has given us the "will" (Phil 2:13) will bestow also the ability, so that we might be cooperators *(cooperatores)* with his works. . . . When we consider, dearly beloved, the ineffable generosity of God in his gifts to us, we should be cooperators *(cooperatores)* with the grace of God "working in us." (Phil 2:13)[13]

Leo is probably dependent on Augustine for this interpretation of Philippians 2:12–13. Wrestling with the meaning of Jesus' promise in John 14:12, that the disciple will do greater works than Jesus himself, Augustine asks in wonder what these works could possibly be. He concludes that Christ is referring to the justification of the ungodly, which is properly the work of Christ, but done in such a way that it is also the work of the one justified:

> In this work let us do the works of Christ, because to believe in Christ is also itself a work of Christ. But he works this in us, surely not without us. . . . Does he do works greater than all those of Christ, he who works out his very own salvation with fear and trembling? But surely Christ works this in him, but not without him. . . . And surely it is a lesser thing to preach the words of justice, which he did apart from us, than to justify the ungodly, which he does in us in such a way that we do it also.[14]

---

[13] *Serm.* 26. 4; Freeland, 108, adjusted; *Serm.* 35. 3; Freeland, 152.

[14] *Trac. in Io.* 72. 2–3; Rettig, vol. 90, 82–83.

In his own statement of the matter, Aquinas accepts and develops Augustine's perspective. Concerning human salvation, he upholds the principle that "what is produced in me by God is also produced in me by myself, that is, by my free choice *(liberum arbitrium)*,"[15] but he states clearly that our free cooperation is itself a result of grace:

> God does not justify us without ourselves, because while we are being justified we consent to God's justification by a movement of our free-will. Nevertheless this movement is not the cause of grace, but the effect; hence the whole operation pertains to grace.[16]

In his lectures on justification, John Henry Newman speaks with the same voice as Leo, Augustine, and Aquinas about the great gift of becoming cooperators with God:

> This is what I have been hitherto saying, but this is not all—*with* His grace we are gifted not only with the capacity of being led into truth and holiness, but with the power of co-operating with Him. . . . [God's grace] enables us to obey, not as instruments merely, but as free agents, who, while they obey, are not constrained to obey, except that they choose to obey.[17]

In a theological *apologia* for the position adopted by Augustine on this question, Hans Urs von Balthasar states why the collaboration of the creature with God is inherent in God's purpose of salvation:

> It is meaningless to attempt to exclude carefully every collaboration of the creature's freedom within the indwelling divine freedom, in order to avoid any appearance of synergism. For God's affirmation of his creature in the accomplishment of his covenant does not in the least aim at bringing the powers of the creature to silence and replacing them: rather, his aim is to empower them through the indwelling of his own working to an activity that lies beyond any capacity of their own for working.[18]

---

15 *Comm. in. Io.* 14:8–14 [1900]; Weisheipl, 349.

16 *Summa theologiae* I–II, q. 111, a. 2, reply 2.

17 *Lectures on Justification,* 95.

18 *The Glory of the Lord,* vol. 7, 310–11

Kallistos Ware, employing the distinctive idiom of the Eastern tradition, describes human cooperation with divine grace (called *synergeia*) in a way that displays many of the same elements we have identified in the Western tradition:

> Created as we are in God's image and likeness, we have been endowed with the divine quality of freedom. God created us free, and Christ has restored that freedom to us (Gal 5:1). We *cannot* be saved without God's grace, but God *will* not save us without our voluntary consent. . . . In no sense is grace a reward for works, yet at the same time "faith without works is dead" (Jas 2:17). Salvation and *theosis* involve, therefore, the convergence of two factors, unequal in value but both equally necessary: divine grace and human freedom. What God does is incomparably more important that what man does, yet man's participation is also indispensable.[19]

As Orthodox scholar John Behr states more succinctly: "Thus, in the case of human beings, salvation and deification is neither a result of human action nor is it a mechanical procedure, for it requires our total and active cooperation to make our own what is offered in Christ."[20]

To sum up, our deification in Christ is grounded in the saving initiative of God in Christ through the Holy Spirit, and all progress in deification is based upon what God has already done to make us "sons in the Son," temples of the Holy Spirit, and partakers of the divine nature. But by his freely given grace, we are enabled to respond freely to him and cooperate with his ongoing work. It is the peculiar quality of divine grace that it calls and enables the creature to cooperate fully and freely in its transformation into Christ.

Transformation into the Image of Christ

It is difficult to find a loftier or more eloquent statement in the Scriptures concerning our destiny in Christ than what Paul writes in 2 Corinthians 3:18 and Romans 8:28–29. In the first passage, transformation into "the same image" is revealed as the endpoint of the greater glory made available in the New Covenant: "And we all, with unveiled

[19] "Salvation and Theosis in Orthodox Theology," 179–80.
[20] *The Nicene Faith,* vol. 1, 231.

face, beholding the glory of the Lord, are being transformed into the same image from one degree of glory to another; for this comes from the Lord who is the Spirit" (RSV, adjusted). In the second passage, conformity to the image of God's Son is shown to be the eternal purpose of God for us in Christ: "For those whom he foreknew he also predestined to be conformed to the image of his Son, in order that he might be the first-born among many brethren." In both texts, the term "image" is critical. A brief account, then, of how the term "image" is used in the Bible (and with it, the parallel term, "likeness") will help us grasp the depth of what Paul is describing as our destiny in Christ.

The first thing to strike someone who tracks down the biblical use of the terms "image" and "likeness" is how *infrequently* they appear in the Bible to describe human status before God. The only positive use of these terms in the Old Testament to describe our relationship to God—aside from three references in Wisdom and Sirach[21]—is found in the first nine chapters of Genesis.[22] Genesis 1:26–27 is foundational, and all other uses of "image" and "likeness" to refer to our status before God are based upon this text. "Then God said, 'Let us make man in our image, after our likeness; and let them have dominion.' . . . So God created man in his own image, in the image of God he created him; male and female he created them." The two terms, "image" (Hebrew, *selem*; Greek, *eikōn*; Latin, *imago*) and "likeness" (Hebrew, *demut*; Greek, *homoiōsis*; Latin, *similitudo*), appear to be used synonymously in Genesis 1:26–27. But there is a long-standing discussion in the Christian tradition as to whether the terms "image" and "likeness" refer to the same reality or to distinct aspects of our created status before God. On the one side of this issue are authorities such as Athanasius, Hilary, Cyril of Alexandria, and Augustine, who hold that there is no significant difference between the terms "image" and "likeness" in the Scripture.[23] The Western theological tradition, following Augustine, has typically understood "image" and "likeness" to be roughly synonymous terms. The patristic witness to the other side of this issue—that the terms "image" and "likeness" refer to

21 Wis 2:23, 7:26; Sir 17:3.

22 Gen 1:26–27, 5:1, 3, 9:6.

23 The terms "image" and "likeness" are equivalents in Athanasius (Behr, *The Nicene Faith,* vol. 1, 190), in Hilary of Poitiers (Russell, *The Doctrine of Deification,* 328), and in Cyril and Augustine (Burghardt, *The Image of God,* 7–11).

distinguishable aspects of the divine work in us—begins with Irenaeus,[24] and is developed by authorities such as Clement of Alexandria, Evagrius, Diadochus, and Maximus the Confessor.[25] According to this view, "image" refers to what is given in creation and not lost in the Fall, while "likeness" typically describes what the human race lost in the Fall, and what we progressively attain as we cooperate with the grace of God in Christ. The Eastern theological tradition, following Maximus, has typically distinguished the terms "image" and "likeness" along these lines.[26]

On close inspection, the terms "image" and "likeness" in Genesis and in the New Testament do not obviously yield the theological distinction that is sometimes ascribed to them. They appear to be used synonymously and interchangeably. This judgment of course does not invalidate a later theological application of the terms to refer to distinguishable aspects of what was given in creation, lost in the Fall, and

Cyril expresses his firm disagreement with those who make a distinction between the two terms: "If they say that 'according to the image' and 'according to the likeness' are two different things, let them show the difference! For our mind is that 'according to the image' means nothing else than 'according to the likeness,' and conversely 'according to the likeness' means nothing but 'according to the image.'. . . The fact is, it is useless to say that the latter [the likeness] has been reserved for us for the life to come. . . . We shall, it is true, be like Christ in incorruption . . . [but] even now we are not alien to his likeness, if it is really true that he is formed in us through the Holy Spirit." *De dogmatum solutione,* 3; trans. Burghardt, *The Image of God,* 7.

24 *Adv. Haer.* 5. 6. 1. But Irenaeus also appears to use the two terms synonymously as well (*Adv. Haer.* 3. 18 1; 5. 12. 4). For the "conflicted" presentation of image and likeness in Irenaeus, see Jeffrey Finch, "Irenaeus on the Christological Basis of Human Divinization," in *Theōsis: Deification in Christian Theology,* 87–88.

25 According to Maximus: "Thus those things belonging to his essence which display the fact that we are in his image, he has given naturally to the soul. But the other things belonging to the activity of God which indicate likeness to him, these he has left to our self-determining will while he awaits the perfection of man." *Quaestiones et dubia,* III. 1.1–20; trans. Cooper, *The Body in St. Maximus the Confessor,* 98.

26 Representing the Eastern tradition, Kallistos Ware (*The Orthodox Church,* 224) writes: "However sinful a man may be, he never loses the image; but the likeness depends upon our moral choice, upon our 'virtue,' and so it is destroyed by sin." It is ironic that the *Catechism of the Catholic Church,* which sometimes speaks of image and likeness without distinction (e.g., §1602, 1604, 1700, 1701, 2809), also frequently and explicitly distinguishes image from likeness along the lines laid down by Irenaeus and the Eastern tradition (e.g., §705, 708, 720, 734, 2566, 2713, 2784).

regained in Christ. In the end, the difference between the two traditions is not necessarily significant. Both acknowledge that there are distinguishable aspects of what was given in creation, what was lost in the Fall, what was restored in the new creation in Christ, what is worked in us progressively as we cooperate with the grace given in Christ, and what is perfected in us in the life of the age to come.[27]

Whether we equate or distinguish the terms "image" and "likeness," they both have a close affiliation with the notion of "sonship"—and this is the crucial conclusion for our study. To say that we are created "in the image and likeness of God" is to state, most simply, that we are "sons and daughters of God" in a way that is not true of any other created being on earth. In Genesis 5:1 the narrator states that the human race, male and female, was created in the "likeness of God" (the Hebrew Masoretic text has "likeness," the Greek Septuagint "image"), and he goes on in 5:3 to say that Adam in his turn "became the father of a son in his likeness, according to his image." To be made in the image and likeness of someone is most fundamentally to be a "son" or "true offspring." The correlation of "image" with "son" also appears in Luke's genealogy of Jesus, where delightfully God himself is placed in the long line of fathers and sons: "the son of Seth, the son of Adam, the son of God" (Lk 3:38). Adam, made in the image of God, is God's "son"; and Jesus, the New Adam, is the true image, the eternal Son now made man, revealing to us who we are to become as sons and daughters made in the image and likeness of God.

In the New Testament, it is Paul who employs the term "image," first to describe Christ as the true Son of God, and then to identify what we are to become in Christ. The order is significant: Christ is the true and perfect image of the Father; we are called to become conformed to the image that Christ is. Athanasius writes: "In short, [Christ] is the supremely perfect fruit of the Father, and is alone Son, the exact image of the Father."[28] In 2 Corinthians 4:4, Paul speaks of

---

[27] For example, Aquinas, *Summa theologiae* II–II, q. 163, a. 2, identifies different senses of the single term "likeness" *(similitudo)* in a way that approximates how the Eastern tradition distinguishes between "image" and "likeness."

[28] *C. Gentes* 46; trans. Behr, *The Nicene Faith,* vol. 1, 183. For Christ as the true and perfect image of God whose image we bear, see Thomas G. Weinandy, "St. Irenaeus and the *Imago Dei,*" *Logos* 6 (2003): 15–34.

"the light of the gospel of the glory of Christ, who is the image of God," and in Colossians 1:15, he says of "the Beloved Son" (v. 13) that "he is the image of the invisible God." The close kinship between being the "Son" and being the "image" is evident, especially in the latter text.[29] Paul is almost certainly drawing on the description of Adam as the "image" of God in Genesis when he makes these claims about Christ. In 1 Corinthians 15:45–49, he explicitly deploys the Adam–Christ parallel to show how Christ is the New and life-giving Adam, and he concludes by announcing that we are called to bear the image, not of the old Adam, but of the new and heavenly one: "Just as we have borne the image of the man of dust, we shall also bear the image of the man of heaven" (v. 49). We are called to become "sons in the Son" by bearing the image of the Son. This is just what Romans 8:29 affirms: We are "to be conformed to the image of his Son, in order that he might be the first-born among many brethren."[30] As St. Basil writes,

> Therefore, since the Holy Spirit perfects reason-endowed beings, he is present *in* them in the same way that form is present *in* matter. Such a person no longer lives according to the flesh, but is led by the Spirit of God. He is called a son of God, because he is conformed to the image of the Son of God.[31]

Perfect conformity to the image of the Son in both body and soul awaits eternal life and the resurrection of the body, but Paul clearly expects that in this life we will make progress in conforming to the image of Christ. Employing the baptismal imagery of stripping off the

---

29 G. Kittel confirms this conclusion in his article on "eikōn" (image): "The being of Jesus as image [in Col 1:15] is only another way of talking about His being as the Son." *Theological Dictionary of the New Testament,* ed. G. Kittel, trans. Geoffrey Bromiley (Grand Rapids, MI: Eerdmans, 1964), 395.

30 The one and only use of the Greek term *homoiōsis* (likeness) in the New Testament appears in Jas 3:9. James affirms here that the human race has been made in the likeness of its creator. The cognate words, *homoiōma* (likeness/form) and *homoiōo* (to be made like), are used for describing Christ's taking on our likeness in the Incarnation: Rom 8:3 ("the likeness of sinful flesh"); Phil 2:7 ("being born in the likeness of men"); Heb 2:17 ("made like his brethren in every respect").

31 *De Spir.* 26. 61; St. Basil the Great, *On the Holy Spirit* (Crestwood, NY: St. Vladimir's Press, 1980), 93.

old clothing and putting on the new, he speaks in Colossians 3:10 in the present progressive tense about the renewal of the image of God in us: "Do not lie to one another, seeing that you have put off the old nature with its practices and have put on the new nature, which *is being renewed* in knowledge after the image of its creator" (emphasis added). Ongoing progress is also evident in 2 Corinthians 3:18. As we behold the glory of the Lord, we "*are being transformed* into the same image from one degree of glory to another" (emphasis added). Paul plainly has in view an ongoing transformation into the image of God—and this image of God is Christ. As he says to the Galatians: "I am again in travail until Christ be formed in you!" (Gal 4:19).

The eternal son of God has taken on our nature, made like us in every respect (Heb 2:17), in order to reveal what the true image of God was intended to be. The Incarnation of the Son of God presents us with a double disclosure. Not only is the glory of God revealed in the face of Christ (2 Cor 4:6; Jn 14:9), but the true glory of the human race is also revealed. The glory of the true image, however, is not just for our beholding, as if we are limited to gazing upon Christ in wonder. Our beholding him is transformative: "Beloved, we are God's children now; it does not yet appear what we shall be, but we know that when he appears we shall be like him, for we shall see him as he is" (1 Jn 3:2). We are to become what we behold, and we are to make progress in Christ, the image of God, into whom we have already been baptized. Christ is the New Adam, what Adam was intended to be, and we achieve our end in God by being conformed to Christ and transformed into his image.

MATURITY IN CHRIST

The New Testament teaching on "maturity" finds its place in this context. Just as in natural human life we grow from beginnings to maturity, from youth to adulthood, so the Scriptures present life in the kingdom of God as a call to "perfection," which is best understood as maturity in Christ. The biblical words "perfect" (Greek *teleios*) and "perfection" (Greek *teleiotēs*) can mislead us. They do not necessarily convey the kind of flawlessness that is usually associated with the English word "perfect." We know that in this life we are never finished or complete in an absolute way, but are always "pressing on towards the goal" (Phil 3:14) that will find completion only in heaven. Yet we are plainly called to "perfection" in this life in the sense of maturity as sons and daughters of God. Christ himself concludes his teaching on the Law with the summary statement, "You, therefore, must be perfect *(teleioi)*, as your heavenly Father is perfect *(teleios)*" (Mt 5:48). If we hear this with the overtones of the English word "perfect," we are rightly overwhelmed with the Lord's demand. Who can be perfect—without any flaw of any kind—as God is perfect? But the intended sense of "perfect" in Matthew 5:48 is governed by Christ's teaching on the true sense of the Law as outlined in Matthew 5:21–47. By living the true sense of the Law in Christ—and especially by loving our enemies—we show ourselves to be truly sons and daughters of our Father in heaven. "Perfection" in the sense of maturity, then, describes what it means to be sons and daughters of God conformed to the image of Christ.[32]

The analogy between human and spiritual development appears in the Letter to the Hebrews. The author exhorts his hearers to move beyond spiritual infancy and advance to maturity in following Christ: "But solid food is for the mature *(teleioi)*, for those who have their faculties trained by practice to distinguish good from evil. . . . Therefore let us leave the elementary doctrine of Christ and go on to maturity *(teleiotēs)*" (Heb 5:14; 6:1). Paul similarly calls the Corinthians to mature Christian thinking: "Brethren, do not be children in your thinking; be babes in evil, but in thinking be mature *(teleioi)*" (1 Cor 14:20). Indeed, Paul presents the final goal of his apostolic ministry as maturity in Christ: "Him we proclaim, warning every man and teaching every man in all wisdom, that we may present every man mature *(teleios)* in Christ" (Col 1:28). For Paul, the ministries in the Church are given by Christ expressly for this purpose: "until we all attain to

---

32 For Aquinas, "the perfection of the Christian life consists radically in charity" (*Summa theologiae* II–II, q. 184, a. 1), and so consists primarily and essentially in keeping the commandments on the love of God and the love of neighbor—this is incumbent upon all Christians. Secondarily, perfection consists in keeping the evangelical counsels of poverty, chastity, and obedience, which are not enjoined on all, but freely chosen (II–II, q. 184, a.3). He also recognizes a perfection that is possible in this life, even though there is a greater perfection in glory (II–II, q. 184, a.2).

the unity of the faith and of the knowledge of the Son of God, to mature manhood *(andra teleion),* to the measure of the stature of the fullness of Christ" (Eph 4:13).[33] The exhortation to Christian maturity also appears in James, where maturity is the final result of the testing of our faith: "And let steadfastness have its full effect [literally, its "perfect effect," *ergon teleion*], that you may be perfect *(teleioi)* and complete, lacking in nothing" (Jas 1:4).

Christian perfection in a final sense is, of course, attained only in the life of the age to come. Paul makes this clear when he says, "For our knowledge is imperfect and our prophecy is imperfect; but when the perfect *(to teleion)* comes, the imperfect will pass away" (1 Cor 13:9–10). But as we have seen, there is a form of Christian maturity attainable in this life. The gift of the Spirit is given to the Church precisely to bring us into maturity as sons and daughters of God. This yields an important conclusion. By the Spirit we are called to become *mature* sons and daughters of God, spiritual adults, as it were. Christ's call to become like children in order to enter into the kingdom of God (Mt 18:3–4) concerns the virtue of humility. But fundamentally we are called to leave behind spiritual adolescence and become mature sons and daughters, imitating the ways of our Father in heaven and becoming formed in the image of Christ.

GROWTH IN VIRTUE

The Fathers of the Church often speak of Christian maturity and "transformation into the image of Christ" in terms of the acquisition of virtue. This puzzles modern readers, because we do not use the term "virtue" in quite the same way that the earlier Christian tradition did. To us, the term "virtue" conveys a vague sense of moral character, and often has little connection to Christian belief or to the qualities of

---

[33] Most translations of Eph 4:13 render the phrase "perfect man" *(andra teleion)* as "maturity" (e.g., NRSV) or "mature manhood" (e.g., RSV, NAB). But some commentators believe that the phrase refers to Christ himself, the "perfect man." This latter interpretation only strengthens the conclusion that Christian maturity means being conformed to Christ himself, the "perfect man." For this reading, see Markus Barth, *Ephesians 4–6,* The Anchor Bible (Garden City, NY: Doubleday, 1974), 484–87.

faith, hope, and love. Therefore when we encounter a call to pursue virtue in the teaching of the Fathers, we may wonder what this has to do with the distinctives of Christian faith, with grace, and with transformation into Christ. But when they speak in shorthand of growth in virtue, they are in fact referring to our transformation into the image of Christ that comes through our free cooperation with the Spirit.

The opening verses of 2 Peter are instructive in this context. The letter begins by praising the work of the Father, who by his divine power has given us everything that concerns "life and godliness," through the knowledge of Christ, who has called us "to his own glory and excellence [literally, "virtue," *aretē*]." All this enables us to become "partakers of the divine nature" and to escape the corrupting influences of the world (vv. 3–4). On this basis, we are called to "make every effort" to advance in the things that are already given: from faith to "virtue," and then successively to knowledge, to self-control, to steadfastness, to godliness, to brotherly affection, and finally to love (vv. 5–7). This is just one instance of the common New Testament pattern, specified in Paul's writings by opposing lists of virtues and vices (e.g., Rom 13:12–14; Gal 5:19–24; Eph 4:17–32; Col 3:5–17).[34] On the basis of what God has done for us in Christ through the Spirit, we are called to renounce the patterns of our former life and live according to the new way of life in Christ. And so when the Fathers speak of growing in virtue, it is a shorthand way of describing the call to "put off" the former manner of life, and "put on" what pertains to life in Christ.

It is important to recognize that when the Fathers speak of attaining virtue, they are not recommending a path of self-improvement or giving facile acceptance to moral practice in the ancient world. Rather, they are issuing a call to "put on" Christ himself and the new way of life he teaches and models. As Maximus the Confessor says, "There can be no doubt that the one Word of God is the substance of virtue in each person. For our Lord Jesus Christ himself is the sub-

34 For a study of the list of virtues in 2 Pet 1:5–7, and more generally of virtue lists in the New Testament, see J. Daryl Charles, *Virtue Amidst Vice: The Catalog of Virtues in 2 Peter 1,* JSNT Suppl. 150 (Sheffield: Sheffield Academic Press, 1997).

stance of all the virtues."[35] In a wonderful Trinitarian exposition of John 15 (the vine and the branches), Cyril of Alexandria expresses how a life of virtue is the abundant fruit produced by our being attached to Christ the vine through faith and love:

> For just as the root of the vine ministers and distributes to the branches the enjoyment of its own and inherent natural quality, so the only-begotten Word of God, by putting his Spirit within them, imparts to the saints, as it were, a kinship to his own nature and the nature of God the Father, inasmuch as they have been united with him through faith and complete holiness of life; and he nourishes them to godliness, and works in them the knowledge of all virtue and well doing.[36]

Servais Pinckaers goes to the roots of this notion, showing that for Paul transformation by faith must occur if we are to live a life of virtue in Christ:

> Before proud humanity, the would-be center and source of virtue, St. Paul holds up the humiliated Christ, obedient, crucified, risen. To human wisdom and virtue he opposes faith in God through Jesus Christ. . . . Once this foundation is solidly laid, St. Paul, undertaking to describe Christian conduct in daily life, does not hesitate to include the virtues recognized by contemporary Greek culture and to integrate them in his teaching in the light of faith (e.g., Phil 4:8). . . . Faith has worked a transformation in depth and modified these virtues from within.[37]

Likewise, Thomas Aquinas teaches that the attainment of specifically supernatural virtue requires as its prerequisite the new nature in Christ that we have received through grace. Just as the light of natural reason is the basis for the attainment of human virtue, so we need to be born as children of God in order to receive supernatural virtue.

---

[35] Amb. 7; *On the Cosmic Mystery of Jesus Christ: Selected Writings from St. Maximus the Confessor,* trans. Paul M. Blowers and Robert Louis Wilken (Crestwood, NY: St. Vladimir's Press, 2003), 58.

[36] *Comm. In Jo.* 15:1; Pusey, vol. 2, 535–36.

[37] *The Sources of Christian Ethics,* 126–27.

> Infused virtues dispose man in a higher manner and towards a higher end, and consequently in relation to some higher nature, that is, in relation to a participation of the Divine Nature, according to 2 Peter 1:4: "He has given us most great and most precious promises; that by these you may be made partakers of the Divine Nature." And it is in respect of receiving this nature that we are said to be born again sons of God. And thus, even as the natural light of reason is something besides the acquired virtues, which are ordained to this natural light, so also the light of grace which is a participation of the Divine Nature is something besides the infused virtues which are derived from and are ordained to this light.[38]

It is because we have been born anew as sons and daughters of God and are partakers of the divine nature that we can make progress in godly virtue. Here it will be helpful to employ a distinction, found in Augustine and developed in Leo the Great, between Christ as *sacramentum* ("mystery") and Christ as *exemplum* ("model"). As *sacramentum*, Christ himself accomplishes the work of salvation, cleanses us from sin, and joins us to the Father. As *exemplum* Christ provides the model for how we are to live in him. Leo sums up this double dependence on Christ by stating that "we cannot come to Christ except by Christ," showing that our imitation of him is necessarily founded on our redemption in him.[39] Because Christ has assumed our nature and redeemed it in himself, and given us a participation in him, we can now "put on" the qualities of that new nature in imitation of Christ himself. In this we are active, putting into practice by the grace of Christ the new way of life in Christ.

While virtue in all its forms is the expected fruit of the divine life we have received, it is preeminently faith, hope, and love that mark the mature Christian. This triad, found in Paul and in the Letter to the Hebrews,[40] comprises what the Christian tradition calls the theological virtues, meaning that they derive from God and lead directly to him,

---

38 *Summa theologiae* I–II, q. 110, a. 3.

39 *Serm.* 67. 6; Freeland, 295.

40 The triad of faith, hope, and love can be found in Rom 5:1–5; 1 Cor 13:7, 13; Gal 5:5–6; Col 1:3–5; 1 Th 1:2–3, 5:8; and Heb 10:19–25. See also Augustine's classic work, *The Enchiridion on Faith, Hope and Love.*

and cannot be attained by human effort. Though given by God, they are nonetheless that which the Christian lives by and acts from. To live a mature Christian life, progressively conformed to the image of Christ, is to live by faith, hope, and love. It is no accident that the list of virtues cited above in 2 Peter begins with faith and ends with love. Paul sums up the Christian life as "faith working through love" (Gal 5:6), and sets faith, hope, and love apart from all else (1 Cor 13:13). Yet as Paul stresses in the same text, "the greatest of these is love." Love in particular is the crown of all the virtues, as Paul clarifies when listing the things we are to "put on" in Colossians 3:10–14: "And over all these put on love, that is, the bond of perfection *(teleiotēs)*" (NAB). This text neatly exhibits love as the crown of "perfection," that is, of Christian maturity.

ASCETICISM AND PRAYER

When considering Christian maturity and transformation in Christ, brief mention should be made of both Christian asceticism (what the Eastern tradition calls *askesis*) and prayer. Christian asceticism is nothing other than the performance of what Paul calls "putting off" and "putting on." Because we have been made sons and daughters of God, freed from the sovereignty of sin and the power of the devil, we are enjoined to "put to death the misdeeds of the body" by the Spirit (Rom 8:13), and to "resist the devil" (Jas 4:7). Just as Christ, following his baptism and anointing by the Spirit, was led by the same Spirit into the wilderness to be tempted by the devil (Lk 4:1), so are we called to engage in spiritual battle for obedience to the Father and for the keeping of his commands. On the one hand, Christian asceticism is the practice of putting off anger, envy, quarreling, drunkenness, sexual immorality, and the like. On the other, it is the practice of putting on compassion, kindness, lowliness, meekness, patience, forbearance, and love (Col 3:12–14). It is making every effort (2 Pet 1:5) to grow in Christ-like virtue and to "strive . . . for the holiness without which no one will see the Lord" (Heb 12:14). Describing the approach taken by Athanasius to Christian asceticism, John Behr accents the need for the grace of God, but also the correlative need for our struggle:

> Christian asceticism is not simply a work of human beings upon themselves, who, by their own efforts, attempt to transcend their human nature to what they consider divine. Rather, as understood by Athanasius, it reflects the possibility, opened by Christ in his Passion, to have communion with God, and embody the Word. This is a possibility which is only actualized by the free and unconstrained grace of God, but also, as we have seen, only through the free application and struggle of man.[41]

Christian prayer is also an integral part of growth into the image of Christ, and so of growth in deification. The emphasis on growth in deification through mystical prayer is especially strong in monastic writers (e.g., Maximus the Confessor and John of the Cross). It is not possible here to enter into a full discussion of what the Christian tradition calls mystical and contemplative prayer. The point here is simply that growth in prayerful communion with the Father through the Son and in the Holy Spirit is part of our growth in deification. This truth is grounded in the example of Christ himself and his prayerful communion with the Father. If we are "sons in the Son," becoming more and more transformed into the image of Christ, then we too are called to enter into communion with our Father in prayer. Prayer is both a means to our ongoing progress in deification ("beholding the glory of the Lord, we are being transformed into the same image"), and a chief goal and end of our deification. Communion with God and one another is the goal of the divinized life. Through Christ's redeeming work, we are made sons and daughters of God and invited into the Trinitarian communion of love. As with all aspects of our growth in Christ, some will make more progress in prayerful communion with God in this life than others. They show an advanced degree of transformation because of their close communion with God in prayer. And in this they serve as pioneers who prepare the way for the rest of us to follow. But all Christians are called to prayerful communion with God, and all have their destiny in a Trinitarian communion of love.

---

[41] *The Nicene Faith,* vol. 1, 259.

SHARING IN THE SUFFERING AND DEATH OF CHRIST

One could get the impression that deification is marked by continual and upward progress, a simple march "from glory to glory." The terms often used to describe deification—transformation, progress, growth, and transfiguration—help to communicate the sense of continuous advance. The anonymous author of *Orthodox Spirituality* reminds us that it is not always so:

> Deification may be a constant and progressive union. It may also be very intermittent and interrupted by falls. It is not, for the Christian, something extraordinary, but the quite ordinary development and stabilization of the state which man is called to experience after baptism, after Chrismation, after Eucharistic communion and, generally, whenever he adheres to God with his whole heart and with his whole mind. Deification, therefore, is something much simpler and more frequent than is often thought. It admits of various degrees, which represent the growth of Christ in us.[42]

But for reasons far deeper than our tendency to stumble along the way, deification should not be viewed as progress from glory to glory in human terms. Deification cannot be understood apart from the Cross and the call to suffer for the sake of Christ. Following his own baptism and anointing by the Spirit, Jesus was led out into the wilderness to be tested by the devil; following his most powerful miracles he was rejected by many; and following his Transfiguration, he descended to walk the road of the Cross. As it was with our Master and Lord, so it is with us. Our progress in deification is modeled on Christ's life and work, and on his work in us. Just as we begin with baptism, the gift of the Spirit, and communion with Christ's body and blood in the Eucharist, so we continue. Baptism and the Eucharist not only are the gate of entry for the deified life, but they also provide the shape that the deified life in Christ will follow.

Shortly before his Passion, Christ spoke of his upcoming death in terms of baptism: "I have a baptism to be baptized with; and how I

---

[42] *Orthodox Spirituality: An Outline of the Orthodox Ascetical and Mystical Tradition,* 3rd ed. (Crestwood, NY: St. Vladimir's Press, 1987), 98.

am constrained until it is accomplished!" (Lk 12:50). When chastening James and John for seeking positions of power, Jesus announced that they would share in the same baptism that he is to undergo. "But Jesus said to them, 'You do not know what you are asking. Are you able to drink the cup that I drink, or to be baptized with the baptism with which I am baptized?' And they said to him, 'We are able.' And Jesus said to them, 'The cup that I drink you will drink; and with the baptism with which I am baptized, you will be baptized' " (Mk 10:38–39). Then at the Last Supper, Jesus referred the bread and the wine of the Passover meal to his impending sacrificial death, and invited his disciples to commune with his body and blood.

Paul does not say where he received the theology of baptism he offers in Romans 6:3–8, but it is not improbable that he gained it from Christ's words cited above. Paul writes: "Do you not know that all of us who have been baptized into Christ Jesus were baptized into his death?" Our baptism is at root a sacramental participation in Christ's death, burial, and resurrection. In the same way, Paul speaks about our ongoing participation in the body and blood of Christ in the Eucharist: "The cup of blessing which we bless, is it not a participation in the blood of Christ? The bread which we break, is it not a participation in the body of Christ?" (1 Cor 10:16). Our share in Christ's death and resurrection in baptism, and our participation in his sacrificial death through his body and blood in the Eucharist, not only initiates us into the Christian life, but also provides the plan and outline for our life in Christ.[43] It is striking how closely Paul links our divine filiation as "sons of God" with the call to suffer with Christ: "It is the Spirit himself bearing witness with our spirit that we are children of God, and if children, then heirs, heirs of God and fellow heirs with Christ, provided we suffer with him in order that we may also be glorified with him" (Rom 8:16–17).

Paul came to interpret his own life and ministry in just these terms. When giving an account to the Corinthians of the extreme trials

---

43 See *Orthodox Spirituality*, 36–103, for an itinerary of the Christian life based on the sacraments of baptism, chrismation, and the Eucharist. The author, while respecting the traditional threefold division of the Christian life into the purgative, illuminative, and unitive stages, proposes that the sacraments of initiation provide an even more foundational itinerary for the Christian life.

and persecutions he and those with him experienced, he concludes that they are "always carrying in the body the death of Jesus, so that the life of Jesus may also be manifested in our bodies. For while we live we are always being given up to death for Jesus' sake, so that the life of Jesus may be manifested in our mortal flesh. So death is at work in us, but life in you" (2 Cor 4:10–12). Being given up to death for Jesus' sake, and having "death at work in us," does not immediately sound like a description of the deified life. But this is just what we should expect if we understand that deification is being transformed into the image of Christ. As his body, we are called to participate in his suffering and death, just as we are in his resurrection.

In the letter to the Philippians, Paul testifies to his own calling and prays that he may have a share not only in the power of Christ's resurrection, but also in his suffering and death, so that he might know Christ and be found in him.

> But whatever gain I had, I counted as loss for the sake of Christ. Indeed I count everything as loss because of the surpassing worth of knowing Christ Jesus my Lord. For his sake I have suffered the loss of all things, and count them as refuse, in order that I may gain Christ and be found in him, not having a righteousness of my own, based on law, but that which is through faith in Christ, the righteousness from God that depends on faith; that I may know him and the power of his resurrection, and may share his sufferings, becoming like him in his death, that if possible I may attain the resurrection from the dead. (Phil 3:7–11)[44]

Reflecting on the relationship between deification *(theosis)* and the Cross, Kenneth Paul Wesche writes:

> The path to *theosis* is the way of the cross, a journey of the soul into the mystery of Christ's death. There a deeper mystery of the resurrection and eternal life through union with God is discovered. This

[44] For an exegetical and theological study of these two texts, see Michael Byrnes, *Conformation to the Death of Christ and the Hope of Resurrection: An Exegetico-Theological Study of 2 Corinthians 4:7–15 and Philippians 3:7–11* (Rome: Editrice Pontificia Università Gregoriana, 2003).

> is the divine life of the Spirit. . . . *Theosis* is therefore a process of transformation from death in the flesh to life in the divine.[45]

Deification is not a bypassing of the Cross or a passage to glory that avoids sharing in Christ's suffering and death. Because deification means being progressively conformed to the image of Christ, there is no route to this transformation apart from participation in the suffering, death, and resurrection of Christ. Progress in the deified life will always have a baptismal and Eucharistic form.

Conclusion

What does progress in deification mean? It means that we are to become progressively like Christ, transformed into the image of the one who is the very image of God. The more we become conformed to the image of Christ, the more we are like our Father in heaven (Mt 5:48). We are to become holy as he is holy (1 Pet 1:15). It means that we are to grow into mature sons and daughters of God, living a life more and more characterized by the virtues of Christ himself, especially faith, hope, and love. "Therefore be imitators of God, as beloved children. And walk in love, as Christ loved us and gave himself up for us, a fragrant offering and sacrifice to God" (Eph 5:1–2). Through our abiding in Christ and our increasing likeness to him, we are to be fruitful as the Father intended us to be (Jn 15:8).

We can make progress in deification only because God in Christ has redeemed and transformed our nature, and has come to dwell effectively in us through the Spirit. By his grace at work in us, our freedom is revived and strengthened, enabling us to work with him in our own transformation. Further, our progress in deification follows a baptismal and Eucharistic pattern. It will often lack the outward appearance of glory, and it will not always be evident to the wayfarer that he or she is being progressively transformed into the image of Christ. Paradoxically, we advance in the divine life by sharing in Christ's suffering and death, and in the midst of this death, we experience the transforming power of

[45] "Eastern Orthodox Spirituality: Union with God in *Theosis*," *Theology Today* 56 (1999): 30.

his resurrection. "Though our outer nature is wasting away, our inner nature is being renewed every day" (2 Cor 4:16).

A large portion of the biblical witness to our ongoing transformation and deification has been taken from the writings of the Apostle Paul. It may be useful, in closing, to observe how his own life exemplifies the description of progress in deification offered here. Paul, by his own admission, was a zealous persecutor of the first Christians. On the road to Damascus, the risen Christ broke into his life and spoke to him. But this event by itself was not the whole of Paul's initiation into the life of Christ. Lying blind for three days in the city, Paul was then visited by Ananias, who spoke to him about receiving his sight and the Holy Spirit, prayed for him, and then baptized him (Acts 9:17–18). Immediately following this we hear of Paul testifying powerfully to the Lordship of Christ. It was not only the heavenly vision, then, but also the gift of the Holy Spirit in baptism that inaugurated new life in Christ for Paul. In his letters, Paul repeatedly speaks of the gift of the indwelling Spirit as the principle of the New Covenant life—a gift that he plainly experienced in his own conversion and throughout his life.

Paul gives eloquent witness to the transformation worked in his life by the grace of God, conforming him to Christ: "I have been crucified with Christ; it is no longer I who live, but Christ who lives in me; and the life I now live in the flesh I live by faith in the Son of God, who loved me and gave himself for me" (Gal 2:20). This plainly did not come about in Paul's life without practical Christian asceticism: "Every athlete exercises self-control in all things. They do it to receive a perishable wreath, but we an imperishable. Well, I do not run aimlessly, I do not box as one beating the air; but I pommel my body and subdue it, lest after preaching to others I myself should be disqualified" (1 Cor 9:25–27). Paul was also aware of the great fruitfulness that his life and ministry produced. He attributed this to the grace of God, not his own competency (2 Cor 3:5–6), but nonetheless acknowledged the place of his own efforts in serving the Lord: "For I am the least of the apostles, unfit to be called an apostle, because I persecuted the church of God. But by the grace of God I am what I am, and his grace toward me was not in vain. On the contrary, I worked harder than any of them, though it was not I, but the grace of God which is with me" (1 Cor 15:9–10).

Paul also experienced deep communion with Christ in prayer and speaks to the Philippians about his desire to be with Christ: "For to me to live is Christ, and to die is gain. If it is to be life in the flesh, that means fruitful labor for me. Yet which I shall choose I cannot tell. I am hard pressed between the two. My desire is to depart and be with Christ, for that is far better" (Phil 1:21–23). And we have already seen how Paul embraced the frequent sufferings that attended his apostolic ministry as a share in the suffering, death, and resurrection of Christ. Paul was most probably not a flawless or faultless man, but he was a mature Christian disciple whose life and writings present us with a concrete portrait of deified life in Christ.

CHAPTER FIVE

Partakers of the Divine Nature

It is evident, then, as he has called men gods, that they are deified by his grace, not born of his substance. . . . If we have been made sons of God, we have also been made gods: but this is the effect of grace adopting, not of nature generating.

—Augustine of Hippo, *Enar. in Ps.* 49.2

WE HAVE NOW examined in some detail the meaning of deification according to the "formula of exchange" *(admirabile commercium)*: how Christ has redeemed and deified our nature in himself (chapter two); how we have become "sons" and "gods" by receiving new life through the effective indwelling of God (chapter three); and how we make progress in the divine life through transformation into the image of Christ (chapter four). It is now time to return to a question that was posed at the start: Does the doctrine of deification, by means of its elevated and potentially exaggerated rhetoric, effectively compromise the fundamental distinction between God and the created order, and so lead explicitly or implicitly to a form of pantheism? To restate the question against the backdrop of contemporary religious movements: Doesn't the notion of deification play into the hands of those religious movements that claim, "you yourself are God," and so refuse to recognize any sovereign and transcendent God deserving of our worship and obedience? The answer given by the Christian tradition is a resounding "No." These concerns are not new—they were present from the very beginning of discussion of deification in the Church. Clear distinctions were set in place to ensure that talk of deification would not fall prey to pantheism or fail to uphold the transcendence of the divine nature. Properly understood, the Christian doctrine of deification not only maintains the distinction between God and the created order, but is premised on it. Christian deification dissolves if the fundamental difference between what is divine and what is human is compromised.

CALLED TO BE GODS, NOT BY NATURE, BUT BY GRACE

The primary statement in the Christian tradition that upholds this difference takes some form of the saying "we become gods, not by nature, but by grace." A chorus of voices attesting to this—ancient, medieval, and modern—will help us grasp how widespread is the conviction that deification does not compromise divine transcendence, but rather reveals the divine plan for the glorification of human nature in the Incarnate Son. We begin once again with Irenaeus, who attests to our becoming gods by the grace of adoption: "But of what gods [does he speak]? [Of those] to whom he says, 'I have said, you are gods, and all sons of the Most High' (Ps 82:6) To those, no doubt, who have received the grace of the adoption, 'by which we cry, Abba Father' " (Rom 8:15).[1] Two centuries later Athanasius echoes Irenaeus, but adds the distinction between the Word, who is God in essence, and human beings, who are "gods" by participation: "Wherefore [the Word] is very God, existing one in essence with the very Father; while other beings, to whom he said, 'I said you are gods' (Ps 82:6), had this grace from the Father, only by participation of the Word, through the Spirit."[2] Cyril of Alexandria follows Athanasius closely, stating that we are destined to be "gods by grace,"[3] and displaying at one and the same time both the grandeur and the proper ontological boundary of the deification of human nature in Christ:

> Do you hear how the only-begotten Word of God became like us, that we too might become like him so far as is possible for human

1 *Adv. Haer.* 3. 6. 1; ANF, vol. 1, 418.

2 *C. Ar.* 1. 9; NPNF, 2nd series, vol. 4, 311. See also *C. Ar.* 1. 37; 3. 17, 19; *Ep. Serap.* 2. 4.

3 *Comm. In Jo.* 6:15; Pusey, vol. 1, 423.

> nature and to the extent that may be ascribed to the renewal through grace? For he humbled himself that he might raise up that which is humble by nature to his own stature, and he put on the form of a servant although he was by nature Lord and Son, that he might transfer what was servile by nature to the glory of adopted sonship, according to his own likeness. . . . Therefore he became like us, that is, a human being, that we might become like him, I mean gods and sons. On the one hand he accepts what belongs to us, taking it to himself as his own, and on the other he gives us in exchange what belongs to him.[4]

John Chrysostom follows the same path. Commenting on Romans 8:29, that we are destined "to be conformed to the image of his Son," he states: "See what superb honor! For what the Only-begotten was by nature, this they also have become by grace."[5]

Ambrose adds the testimony of the West that we become sons of God, not by nature, but by grace:

> The Apostle says that even we shall reign together with Christ in the kingdom of Christ: "If we are dead with Him, we shall also live with Him; if we endure, we shall also reign with Him" (2 Tim 2:11–12). But we by adoption, he by power; we by grace, he by nature.[6]

St. Augustine is particularly eloquent on this point. He consistently states that our share in the divine life—by grace and not by nature—is distinct from Christ's natural divinity.

> It is evident, then, as he has called men gods, that they are deified by his grace, not born of his substance. . . . If we have been made sons of God, we have also been made gods: but this is the effect of grace adopting, not of nature generating.[7]
>
> But let no one believe about the only-begotten Son what he believes about those who were called the children of God according to grace, not nature, as the Evangelist said, "He gave them power to be made children of God" (Jn 1:12). On this same point, the Lord

4 *In Io.* 20:17; trans. Russell, *The Doctrine of Deification,* 199.

5 *Hom. in Rom.* 15. 1; NPNF, 1st series, vol. 11, 453.

6 *De Spir.* III. 20. 157; NPNF, 2nd series, vol. 10, 157.

7 *Enar. in Ps.* 49. 2; cited in Russell, *The Doctrine of Deification,* 331.

> himself recalled what was said in the Law: "I have said, 'you are gods, and all of you sons of the Most High'" (Ps 82:6).[8]

Despite John Cassian's differences with Augustine about certain matters related to grace and predestination, his statement on our adoptive sonship by grace mirrors the Bishop of Hippo's:

> They all had God within them, and were all made sons of God, and all were receivers of God, but in a very different and dissimilar way. For all who believe in God are sons of God by adoption, but the Only-begotten alone is Son by nature.[9]

Leo the Great, speaking of our new birth in the Spirit through grace, also follows the path set by Augustine: "With this power, you who were born of the flesh that is subject to decay can be born again from the Spirit of God and can obtain through grace what you do not have through nature."[10]

The later Byzantine tradition speaks with one voice on adoption and deification being by grace and not by nature. Maximus the Confessor says that we become "gods" through divine grace, but are unchanged in nature.

> For just as having loosed the laws of nature supernaturally he was made low for us without change—a human being as we are, sin alone excepted—so also shall we consequently come to be above because of him—gods as he is by the mystery of grace—altering nothing at all of our nature.[11]

In his typically concise language, John of Damascus describes the healing of our nature by Christ, so that we can become by adoption (a parallel expression to "by grace") what the Incarnate Word is by nature:

---

8 *Trac. in Io.* 54. 2; St. Augustine, *Tractates on the Gospel of John 28–54,* trans. John W. Rettig, *Fathers of the Church,* vol. 88 (Washington, DC: Catholic University of America Press, 1993), 302. See also *Trac. in Io.* 2. 13; 48. 10; *De nat. et grat.* 33. 37; *De Cons. Evan.* 2. 3. 6.

9 *De Incar. Dom.* 5. 4; cited in Donald Fairbairn, *Grace and Christology in the Early Church* (Oxford: Oxford University Press, 2003), 178.

10 *Serm.* 22. 5; Freeland, 85.

11 *Amb.* 7; trans. Cooper, *The Body in St. Maximus the Confessor,* 112.

> He delivered our nature from the sin of our first parent and death and corruption, and became the first-fruits of the resurrection, and made himself the way and image and pattern, in order that we, too, following in his footsteps, may become by adoption what he is himself by nature, sons and heirs of God and joint heirs with him.[12]

Symeon the New Theologian sums this up in a pithy phrase: "How is he not a god by grace and adoption who has put on the Son of God?"[13]

Aquinas speaks in nearly identical language about our destiny as "gods by grace," linking this claim to the central biblical texts on deification. Explaining how and in what sense Christ loved his disciples as the Father loved him (Jn 15:9), Thomas says:

> For [Christ] did not love them to the point of their being gods by nature, nor to the point that they would be united to God so as to form one person with him. But he did love them up to a similar point: he loved them to the extent that they would be gods by their participation in grace—"I say you are gods" (Ps 82:6); "He has granted to us precious and very great promises, that through these you may become partakers of the divine nature" (2 Pet 1:4).[14]

Even Martin Luther says that the grace of God elevates and deifies us as sons of God: "For it is true that a man helped by grace is more than a man; indeed, the grace of God gives him the form of God and deifies him, so that even the Scriptures call him "God" and "God's son."[15]

Contemporary writers on deification follow the path marked out by the Fathers. Deification does not remove us from the creaturely limitations of human nature; rather, it is the glorification and transformation of our nature by a graced participation in God. Speaking in terms of *theosis*, Kallistos Ware puts the matter succinctly:

---

12 *De Fid. Orth.* 4. 13; NPNF, 2nd series, vol. 9, 82.

13 *Hymn* 50, cited in Russell, *The Doctrine of Deification,* 301.

14 *In Io.* 15:9–13 [1999]; Weisheipl, 397.

15 "Sermon on the Day of St. Peter and St. Paul," *Weimarer Ausgabe* 2, 247–48; cited in Kärkkäinen, *One With God,* 47. For Luther's teaching on deification, see Simo Peura, "Christ as Favor and Gift *(donum)*: The Challenge of Luther's Understanding of Justification," in Braaten and Jenson, *Union with Christ,* 50–53.

> The concept of *theosis* will not be correctly understood unless in this context a careful differentiation is made between the levels of nature and grace. . . . Through deification, then, we become god *by grace* or *by status (kata charin, kata thesin)*, but not god *by nature (kata physin, kat'ousian)*. We are all of us to be sons of God by grace, but Christ alone is Son of God by nature.[16]

Speaking from the Western theological tradition, Eric Mascall delineates both poles of deification: While fully remaining human beings, we are transported by grace to a new supernatural level of life in God.

> Christian theologians, from the Fathers to the present day, have been explicit that even at the heights of mystical union with the Creator the creature does not lose his creaturely status; the one thing that he cannot undergo is an entitative transformation into the substance of God. Yet they have been equally convinced that no term less than "deification" is adequate to describe the condition of the human being who has been taken by grace into the supernatural realm.[17]

When the concern about the proper limits of deification is raised, the shorthand answer given by the Christian tradition—that we become "gods, not by nature, but by grace"—is usually deemed sufficient to put to rest fears of pantheism. We plainly do not become "God" in any kind of strict identity. As deified, we remain creatures who depend entirely on God for our being and our life. But what does it mean to say that we become "gods by grace"? Does it have any real theological content, or is it simply a poetic phrase, a purposeful decorative exaggeration, meant to lift our minds to the destiny that is ours in Christ? And if it has theological import, does the qualifying phrase, "not by nature," really do the job of securing the proper distinction between God and creation? Just as we investigated (in chapter two) how the formula of exchange is a shorthand way of summing up the entire economy of God in Christ through the Spirit, so here we need to seek greater clarity about how the phrase "gods, not by nature,

16 "Salvation and Theosis," 176.

17 *The Importance of Being Human*, 64.

but by grace," provides a summation both of our privileged destiny in Christ and of the proper ontological understanding of that destiny.

The Concept of Participation

In the Church Fathers. The concept of participation is the primary means by which the Fathers sought to describe how we are "gods, not by nature, but by grace," and to state how we as limited creatures share in the being and life of God. In the thought-world of the Fathers, "participation" and its cognate words (participate, partake, share, etc.) had a more definite meaning than they do for us today. They inherited a common philosophical understanding of these terms—derived from Plato, Aristotle, and the Neo-Platonists—and they re-fashioned them to describe a specifically Christian understanding of God, creation, and redemption in Christ.[18] The concept of participation was used philosophically in two main senses. First, it described how different particulars all share some common element. For example, all individual human beings share a common humanity, and so "partake" of a common nature. In this case each human being shares in this nature equally. Second (and crucially for our purposes) the concept of participation was used to describe the unequal relationship between what is essential and what is derivative. If a king is understood to have authority in himself, then his first minister would participate in that authority. More significantly, if God is the source of all being, then we as creatures participate in his being. We do not share or participate in the divine being as God himself possesses it. Rather, we share in his being in that he gives us our created being by bringing us into existence. He has it essentially; we have it derivatively and by participation. He is being; we participate in being. Participation is a way of speaking about how "in him we live and move and have our being" (Acts 17:28).

It is important to identify the characteristics of this second use of the concept of participation. When used in this way, participation

[18] On the Christian appropriation and transformation of this vocabulary, see David L. Balás, *ΜΕΤΟΥΣΙΑ ΘΕΟΥ: Man's Participation in God's Perfection according to St. Gregory of Nyssa* (Rome: Herder, 1966). For a brief survey of the Greek philosophical background to participation, see Keating, *The Appropriation of Divine Life in Cyril of Alexandria,* 146–47.

necessarily requires a relation between two things that are unequal and that remain unequal and distinct in the act of the one participating in the other. It makes no sense to say that something participates in itself (or that someone participates in oneself). If something simply *becomes* another thing, then it no longer can be said to participate in that thing. Therefore, if we say that something participates in another, then by the definition of the term it is derivative of and dependent on that other. As creatures our very identity is grounded in our dependence on God. We do not have an existence of our own apart from our participation in God. Consequently, participation entails (and guarantees) both a true relation and a real distinction. To sum up, the two basic principles of the concept of participation as found in the Fathers and in the Christian tradition are: (1) that which participates is necessarily distinct (and distinct in kind) from that which is participated in; (2) that which participates possesses the quality it receives only in part; that which is participated in necessarily possesses that quality fully and by nature.

The Fathers repeatedly employ the concept of participation to show that the Son and the Spirit are not creatures, but fully divine, and to distinguish how the Word is Son by nature from how we are "sons" by grace. Athanasius is foremost among those who use this mode of argumentation:

> [The Son is] not a creature or work, but an offspring proper to the Father's essence. Wherefore he is very God, existing one in essence with the very Father; while other beings, to whom he said, "I said you are gods" (Ps 82:6), had this grace from the Father, only by participation of the Word, through the Spirit. . . . For he is himself the Father's power and wisdom, and by partaking of him things originate are sanctified in the Spirit; but the Son himself is not Son by participation, but is the Father's own offspring.[19]

Likewise, Augustine characteristically uses the notion of participation to identify the difference between God and all creation, and to mark the boundary between what Christ the Son of God is by nature from what we are by grace. Commenting on John 5:26, "For as the Father

[19] *C. Ar.* 1. 9; 3. 1; NPNF, 2nd series, vol. 4, 311, 394, adjusted.

has life in himself, so he has granted the Son also to have life in himself," he writes:

> How is the Son life, and how is he having life? He is what he has. You are one thing, you have another thing. For instance, you have wisdom. Are you wisdom itself? Accordingly, because you yourself are not what you have, if you lose what you have, you go back to the state of not having. . . . Not so is God, the Son of God, the Word of the Father. . . . He has wisdom in such a way that he himself is wisdom and makes [men] wise; he has life in such a way that he himself is life and makes [men] alive.[20]

Passages similar to these could be multiplied from the writings of the Fathers and from the main authors of the Byzantine tradition and the medieval West. The following selection from Aquinas is typical of the way that he relates and distinguishes the Word, who is Son by nature, from human beings, who have adoptive sonship through participation and grace:

> If we consider what is proper to the Son as Begotten, and consider the way in which this sonship is attributed to him, that is, through nature, we say that he is the Only-begotten of God: because, since he alone is naturally begotten by the Father, the Begotten of the Father is one only. But if we consider the Son, insofar as sonship is conferred on others through a likeness to him, then there are many sons of God through participation. And because they are called sons of God by a likeness to him, he is called the First-born of all. "Those whom he foreknew, he predestined to become conformed to the image of his Son, so that he might be the First-born of many brothers" (Rom 8:29).[21]

A further distinction is normally drawn between our participation in God in the order of being (ontological participation) and in the order of grace (supernatural participation). In the first, we have our

---

20 *Trac. in Io.* 48. 6; Rettig, vol. 88, 232–33. Aquinas offers a similar interpretation of Jn 5:26, using the concept of participation to distinguish the Son, who has life in himself, from human beings, who have life in the Son by participation: *Comm. Jn.* 5:26 [782].

21 *Comm. Jn.* 1:14 [187]; Weisheipl, 92.

very being through participation in God—and this is true of all created beings. This is what we have "by nature" (our human nature) from the sheer gratuity of God. In the second, human beings, made in the image and likeness of God, participate in the life and qualities of God through Christ and in the Spirit. This is what we possess "by grace." It is on the basis of this distinction that Aquinas says, "Consequently the perfection of the rational creature consists not only in what belongs to it in respect of its nature, but also in that which it acquires through a supernatural participation of Divine goodness."[22] "Deification," then, is a term that describes specifically our supernatural participation in God. Conformed into the likeness of the Son through the Spirit, we become adopted sons and daughters of the Father, and share in the divine life of God. Supernatural participation is not less real than our participation in being; rather, it is of a different order, and indeed, a more elevated and privileged participation in God. It is a personal participation in God—through grace we enter into the personal communion of love of the Father, Son, and Holy Spirit.

> Intimate as is the activity of God at the ontological root of our being, by which he keeps us in existence and energizes our nature, far more intimate is his activity in us in the supernatural order. We might express the contrast by saying that in the natural order God gives us *our* selves, while in the supernatural order he gives us *his* self.[23]

The Biblical Foundation. Though an array of terms was used in the Greek philosophical tradition to refer to participation,[24] the two primary word groups adopted by the Church Fathers are (1) *metochē* (participation) / *metochos* (partaker) / *metechein* (partake), and (2) *koinōnia* (communion) / *koinōnos* (sharer/partaker) / *koinōnein* (share/partake).[25] Though it is possible to distinguish slight differences between the two

[22] *Summa theologiae* II-II, q. 2, a. 3.
[23] Mascall, *The Importance of Being Human,* 65.
[24] The most common term in Plato for participation, *methexis,* does not appear in the New Testament.
[25] The Latin equivalents (placed in parentheses) to the Greek words used for participation in the Bible are: *metochē (participatio); metochos (particeps, socius); metechein (participare); koinōnia (communicatio, communio, societas, participatio); koinōnos (socius, consors, particeps); koinōnein (communicare).*

word groups, they tend to be used interchangeably. It is significant that all these terms and many of their compounds appear in the New Testament, and further are often found in contexts relating to our share in God through Christ and in the Holy Spirit.[26] Though these terms as found in the New Testament do not have a technical philosophical meaning, they nonetheless provide the foundation for understanding our share in the divine life in terms that provide a bridge to the more developed notion of participation in the Church Fathers. In other words, when the Fathers used the concept of participation to describe how we are "sons" and "gods" by grace, they understood themselves to be describing and extending what the Scriptures already said about our communion with God.

It is noteworthy that both parts of the "formula of exchange"—the Son became like us, so that we might become like the Son—are expressed in the New Testament in terms of participation. In Hebrews 2:14 the Incarnation itself is depicted in the language of participation: "Since therefore, the children share *(koinōnein)* in flesh and blood, he himself likewise partook *(metechein)* of the same [nature]." Here we have an example of the first sense of participation, namely, sharing in a common nature. In order to redeem us and "to bring many sons to glory" (Heb 2:10), the Son of God came to share fully in our nature, that is, he became a human being. But the goal of the Son sharing in our nature is also stated in participationist language. We are told in 2 Peter 1:4 that God's divine power at work in us is brought to completion by our becoming "partakers *(koinōnoi)* of the divine nature." Here we have in

---

26 The key words for participation (and their compounds) appear in the following New Testament texts: *metochē* (2 Cor 6:14); *metochos* (Lk 5:7; Heb 1:9, 3:1, 14, 6:4, 12:8); *metechein* (1 Cor 9:10, 12, 10:17, 21, 30; Heb 2:14, 5:13, 7:13); *summetochos* (Eph 3:6, 5:7); *koinōnia* (Acts 2:42; Rom 15:26; 1 Cor 1:9, 10:16; 2 Cor 6:14, 8:4, 9:13, 13:13; Gal 2:9; Phil 1:5, 2:1, 3:10; Phil 1:6; Heb 13:16; 1 Jn 1:3, 1:6, 7); *koinōnos* (Mt 23:30; Lk 5:10; 1 Cor 10:18, 20; 2 Cor 1:7, 8:23; Phil 1:17; Heb 10:33; 1 Pet 5:1; 2 Pet 1:4); *koinōnein* (Rom 12:13, 15:27; Gal 6:6; Phil 4:15; 1 Tim 5:22; Heb 2:14; 1 Pet 4:13; 2 Jn 11); *sukkoinōnein* (Eph 5:11; Phil 4:14; Rev 18:4); *sukkoinōnos* (Rom 11:17; 1 Cor 9:23; Phil 1:7; Rev. 1:9). Other terms for participation in the New Testament, also found in the Greek philosophical tradition, are *metalambanein* (Acts 2:46, 24:25, 27:33; 2 Tim 2:6; Heb 6:7, 12:10) and *metalēpsis* (1 Tim 4:3).

bold and demonstrative language the promise that the Father has sent the Son to deliver us from sin and to cause us to become sharers in the divine nature itself. But in 2 Peter 1:4 we have an example of the second sense of participation, the unequal and derivative sharing by the creature in the infinite Creator. In this case, we as partakers never become, strictly speaking, what we partake of. We partake of the divine life, but we do not become God by nature. And so we can rephrase the formula of exchange ("the Son of God became the Son of Man, so that the sons of men might become sons of God") in terms of the two senses of participation found respectively in Hebrews 2 and 2 Peter 1. The Son of God partook of our nature and became fully what we are (human beings), so that we might partake of the divine nature and become by grace and participation what he is by nature. To put this in the creedal terminology of the Council of Chalcedon (A.D. 451): The eternal Word of God, consubstantial with the Father, became fully a human being, consubstantial with us in our nature, so that we might become partakers of his divinity. But we never become consubstantial (one in being) with the Father as he is; rather, we are inserted by grace into the divine communion of Persons. This is what it means to become "gods by grace."

Among other New Testament texts that employ the vocabulary of participation, three express our relationship to the Holy Spirit in terms of participation: Hebrews 6:4, "partakers *(metochos)* of the Holy Spirit"; 2 Corinthians 13:13, "the fellowship *(koinōnia)* of the Holy Spirit"; and Philippians 2:1, "participation *(koinōnia)* in the Spirit." It is notable that the indwelling of the Spirit, so central to baptism and our divine filiation, is expressed biblically in terms of participation. Obviously we do not *become* the Holy Spirit by virtue of his dwelling within us. We do, however, become partakers of the Spirit, enabling the effective life and power of God to be at work in us, transforming us into the image of Christ and drawing us into the Trinitarian communion of love.

Our share in Christ through the Eucharist is also described in terms of participation. In 1 Corinthians 10:14–22 Paul employs the vocabulary of participation to state the incompatibility between sacrificial pagan meals and the Christian Eucharist. He describes the cup of blessing as "a participation *(koinōnia)* in the blood of Christ," and the bread that is broken as "a participation *(koinōnia)* in the body of Christ." In consequence, we are all one body because we partake *(metechein)* of one bread. He then names those who partake of the sacrifice, whether Israelite or pagan, as "partners" *(koinōnos)* with the one to whom they sacrifice, and concludes that Christians cannot partake *(metechein)* of both the table of the Lord and the table of demons. The terminology of participation, drawn from both word groups, dominates Paul's statement here. In one important sense, we become what we partake of in the Eucharist, namely, the body of Christ. According to Leo the Great, "This partaking *(participatio)* in the body and blood of Christ means nothing else than that we should pass over into what we have taken in."[27] But there remains nonetheless an important distinction between the glorified body of Christ himself and his body that is the Church. As Cyril of Alexandria reminds us, Christ is the very Word of God made flesh, and his body and blood are life-giving. We participate in that life—and so become his body—but our bodies do not thereby become life-giving in turn:

> For it is the body of that which is Life by nature, not of any earthly being. . . . For neither the flesh of Paul (for instance), nor of Peter or any other would work [life] in us; but only and specially that of our savior Christ in whom dwelt all the fulness of deity bodily (Col 2:9).[28]

To sum up, the concept of participation, building on the language of participation in the New Testament, enables us to grasp how we are genuinely related to God and can partake of his life, without jeopardizing the infinite difference that distinguishes the uncreated Trinity from all creatures. As we have seen, participation requires that this difference be maintained—without it, we can no longer speak coherently of us participating in God. But the Patristic understanding of participation also guarantees at the same time that this infinite difference does not keep us distant from God. The transcendence and difference of God is not incompatible with the closest unity and participation, but in fact allows and calls for it. David Bentley Hart articulates how

[27] *Serm.* 63.7; Freeland, 277.

[28] *Comm. in Io.* 6:63; Pusey, vol. 1, 552.

the working-out of the doctrine of the Trinity resolved the seeming contradiction between God's transcendence and his intimate relationship to creation:

> Orthodox Trinitarianism, as it came to be articulated, far from simply absorbing into theology the speculative grammar of the circumambient philosophical culture, overcame the language of metaphysical order to which Christian thought might easily have succumbed, and in so doing arrived, for the first time in Greek thought, at a genuine concept of divine transcendence . . . that the Christian God is at once infinitely more transcendent of and, in consequence, infinitely nearer to (within the very being of) finite reality than was the inaccessible God of antique metaphysics.[29]

It is because God is truly transcendent that he can also be truly immanent, without any confusion. Only because he is genuinely transcendent is it possible for the Son to share our nature fully, without undergoing any change in his divine nature.

In the end, the concept of participation aids us in reading and understanding the scriptural revelation coherently and as a whole. It helps us put together God's transcendence and otherness with the expression of his desire to draw his creation—especially those made in his image and likeness—into the intimate communion that is the Triune God. The Christian doctrine of deification, rightly understood, upholds both of these truths at the same time and depends upon the reality of each. The shorthand phrase, that we are "gods, not by nature, but by grace"—understood in terms of participation—provides then an excellent summary statement of the biblical revelation of the purpose of God for us in Christ.

Participation in the Divine Essence or Energies

When we turn to the question of how to describe this participation in God, we run up against a difference between the East and the West. The Western tradition, following Thomas Aquinas (thirteenth century), speaks about the goal of deification as participation in the

---

[29] *The Beauty of the Infinite,* 182–83.

divine essence, and as culminating in the Beatific vision (the vision of God as he is). The Eastern tradition, following Gregory Palamas (fourteenth century), claims that we participate not in the very essence of God himself, but in the divine energies of God. This difference merits some elaboration and assessment.

For Aquinas and the West, to speak of deification at all means that we are making real contact with God himself—and so we participate in his divine nature, that is, his essence, though we never become that essence. We remain human beings who have the privilege of sharing in the life and being of God himself, and of seeing him as he is in the life of the age to come. In reply to the question, whether human happiness consists in the knowledge of the divine essence, Aquinas answers:

> Final and perfect happiness can consist in nothing else than the vision of the Divine Essence. . . . Consequently, for perfect happiness the intellect needs to reach the very Essence of the First Cause. And thus it will have its perfection through union with God as with that object, in which alone man's happiness consists.[30]

This claim, however, is carefully guarded by the reminder that our participation in God's essence is sheer gift, and that we never come to know God as he knows himself. Thomas says that we see the divine essence, but only God actually comprehends his own essence.[31] In other words, we have real contact with God as he is, but we do not fully comprehend him. He remains always beyond what we can know, and our communion with God is always by way of a partial, creaturely participation. Aquinas's position—knowledge, but not comprehension—reflects Paul's paradoxical prayer for the Ephesians, that they may "know the love of Christ which surpasses knowledge," and so may be "filled with all the fullness of God" (Eph 3:19).

In the Eastern view, to say that we participate directly in the essence of God is to threaten divine transcendence. In order to uphold the claim that we participate in God himself, and yet to preserve the

---

30 *Summa theologiae* I-II, q. 3, a. 8.

31 Ibid., reply 2: "So then the happiness of God, who, in understanding his essence, comprehends it, is higher than that of a man or angel who sees it indeed, but comprehends it not."

fundamental unknowability of God in himself, the East developed the distinction between God's essence and his energies. This view is well represented by Kallistos Ware:

> Deification signifies participation in the divine energies, but not in the divine essence. . . . Fundamentally the terms "grace" and "divine energies" both denote one and the same reality: God in action, transmitting his power and life directly to human persons. . . . The essence-energies distinction makes it possible to assert a genuine mystical "touching" between God and man, while at the same time avoiding pantheism.[32]

According to George Maloney, a Western theologian who favors the Eastern approach, "this doctrine makes it possible to understand how the Trinity can remain incommunicable in essence, and yet dwell within us according to the promise of Christ. When one receives the deifying energies, one receives the indwelling of the Holy Trinity."[33] Linked to the difference between essence and energies is the question of uncreated and created grace. Palamas and the Eastern tradition are typically understood as teaching that we participate not in a created effect, but in uncreated grace, which is God himself in his divine energies. Aquinas and the Scholastic tradition are often characterized as emphasizing the created effect of grace in us, and sometimes caricatured as presenting grace in such a way that we are removed from any real direct contact with God himself.

Both positions, Eastern and Western, are attempting to grapple with what A. N. Williams calls the two poles of deification.

> This simultaneous emphasis on the unbreachable divide between creature and Creator and on the creature's likening to the Utterly Other we will refer to as the two poles of deification. What is most characteristic of a doctrine of deification is the delicate balancing and negotiation of these two themes.[34]

---

32 "Salvation and Theosis," 176–78.

33 *The Undreamed Has Happened: God Lives within Us* (Scranton: University of Scranton Press, 2003), 168.

34 *The Ground of Union: Deification in Aquinas and Palamas* (Oxford: Oxford University Press, 1999), 28.

Each position is seeking to uphold at one and the same time that we have real communion with God himself and that he remains distinct, transcendent, and incomprehensible even as we participate in him. Are the Eastern and Western positions in fundamental conflict? Williams argues that despite real differences, the two approaches uphold the same fundamental truths concerning human participation in the divine life.[35] The Western view asserts that we attain to participation in God's essence, but then qualifies this to guard divine transcendence and difference. If Aquinas accents the created effects of grace in us, he is no less clear that it is the Holy Spirit who dwells within us as the constant source of all the created effects of grace and our transformation into the image of Christ.[36] Conversely, the Eastern view insists that the divine energies are not a substitute for God, but God's self-manifestation in the world. By virtue of our participation in the divine energies, we really participate in God himself, but at the same time his essence remains beyond our reach.[37] In the end, both positions are attempting to maintain the biblical revelation concerning our real participation in the divine life through Christ in the Spirit, while fencing off any suggestion of pantheism. Hans Urs von Balthasar sums up the matter well: "No matter how deeply God will initiate us, too, into his divine life, we will never pass from being creatures to being God."[38]

---

35 Ibid, 175: "The ground that Aquinas and Palamas share is vast compared to the points at which they diverge, and considered in context, even their divergences do not reveal diametrical oppositions. One does not, therefore, need to choose between them, for in thinking with either one, one does not reject the shape the doctrine takes in the other."

36 For the predominance of uncreated grace in Aquinas, see Williams, *The Ground of Union,* 82–89, and Keating, "Justification, Sanctification and Divinization in Thomas Aquinas," in *Aquinas on Doctrine: A Critical Introduction*, ed. Thomas Weinandy, Daniel Keating, and John Yocum (London: Continuum/T&T Clark, 2004), 139–58.

37 Kallistos Ware ("Salvation and Theosis," 177) defends the Eastern view against the charge that the essence-energies distinction dissolves divine simplicity: "Likewise, the energies are not a part or subdivision of God, but the one indivisible God in the fullness of his self-manifestation. . . . Thus on the Orthodox view the essence-energies distinction in no way undermines the doctrine of divine simplicity."

38 *Credo: Meditations on the Apostles' Creed,* trans. David Kipp (New York: Crossroad, 1990), 38.

CONCLUSION: PARTAKERS OF THE DIVINE NATURE

I have sought to provide an answer to the question: Does deification threaten the proper distinction between God and his creation, and so lead directly or indirectly to some form of pantheism? By maintaining the distinction between the Son, who is God by nature, and creaturely sons and daughters, who are called to be "gods by grace," the Fathers upheld the truth of our deification in Christ, yet guarded against any taint of pantheism. By means of the concept of participation (in the sense of an asymmetrical relationship between God and creatures), both poles of deification are able to be maintained: We genuinely participate in the divine life, but remain creatures, distinct from God, in the very act of participation. In one sense the explanation thus far has taken up a defensive posture by showing how the proper ontological boundaries between God and creation are not breached by the claims of the Christian doctrine of deification. It is appropriate, therefore, that we also give attention to the positive aspects of what it means to say that in Christ we are called to become "partakers of the divine nature." Through a renarration of the plan of salvation from Adam to Christ, with participation in God as the endpoint, the positive theological content of the doctrine of divinization may become more evident.

The story of the Fall of our race as it comes to us in Genesis is marked by the ironic promise made by the serpent to Eve: "When you eat of [the fruit] your eyes will be opened, and you will be like God" (Gen 3:5). Just as the devil would later tempt Christ, the Second Adam, with a distorted view of his divine sonship ("If you are the Son of God," Mt 4:3), so he beguiles Eve with a distorted account of God's purpose ("If you eat, you will be like God"). There is a certain truth lodged in the serpent's words. It was indeed the purpose of God that the human race become like God. This is what it means to be made in the image and likeness of God. In this respect the devil's seduction was especially effective. He dressed up the path to disobedience with a promise that represented God's true purpose for our race. But instead of attaining to likeness to God through obedience and fear of the Lord as we were intended to do, we set out on our own path to "become like God," imitating the disobedience of the devil, and reaping the fruit of death instead of partaking of the tree of life.

The Incarnation is the appearance of the true Son of God, the image of the invisible God, in human form (Phil 2:5ff). As we have seen, the purpose of the Incarnation was not simply to accomplish a rescue work on behalf of our race, but also to transform our own humanity from within and make it a fit dwelling place for God in the Spirit. By his obedience (Phil 2:8; Heb 5:8) Christ showed himself to be the true Adam, calling and enabling us to become like him: "Just as we have borne the image of the man of dust, we shall also bear the image of the man of heaven" (1 Cor 15:49). In Christ the purpose for the human race, frustrated in Adam, is accomplished. We are to become "like God," transformed into the same image (2 Cor 3:18), and perfected as the "sons of our Father who is in heaven" (Mt 5:45, 48). This can occur only as we abide in Christ as branches in the vine (Jn 15:1ff), and as we are joined in communion *(koinōnia)* "with the Father and his Son Jesus Christ" (1 Jn 1:3).

The centrality of Christ the Incarnate Word merits emphasis here. The process of our deification is entirely dependent on him—not just what he has done, but what he continues to be for us: the locus of our deification. According to the author of *Orthodox Spirituality*, "The process of deification cannot be considered apart from the person of Christ. It is not a metaphysical, a Neoplatonic, deification. It is operated through the Sacred Humanity of our Lord. The Incarnate Christ remains the Alpha and the Omega of our spiritual life."[39] John Meyendorff likewise shows how Christ's own deified humanity is the source and center of our deification in the life of the Church:

> [Christ's humanity] is, therefore, a *deified* humanity, which, however, does not in any way lose its human characteristics. Quite to the contrary. These characteristics become even more real and authentic by contact with the divine model according to which they were created. In this deified humanity of Christ's, man is called to participate, and to share in its deification. This is the meaning of the sacramental life and the basis of Christian spirituality.[40]

---

39 *Orthodox Spirituality*, 99.

40 *Byzantine Theology*, 164.

It has become clear that deification does not mean the change of our nature into something other than it is—it is not an ontological promotion. As Maximus says, "nothing at all changes its nature by being deified."[41] Rather, deification is the transformation and glorification of our nature, so that it can be what God intended it to be: a dwelling place of God in the Spirit. This apparent limitation—that even as deified we remain human beings—is not a defect. It was the devil who desired to supplant God, and in a sense become God as God is, and this is the temptation by which he seduced our race. But the glory intended for the human race is to become "sons" and "gods" by being conformed to the true Son of God, following the path of obedience to the exaltation that God intended and stored up from the beginning: "Therefore God has highly exalted him and bestowed on him the name which is above every name" (Phil 2:9). Therefore, to say that in Christ through the Spirit we become "gods, not by nature, but by grace," is not a concession, a second-best result, leaving us wishing that we could really become sons of God by nature (a thing impossible in any case). If we take on the mind of Christ (Phil 2:5), and not that of the devil, then the so-called limitation, "by grace and not by nature," is in fact our glorious destiny as creatures. We could hope for nothing further than to share as sons and daughters of God—as creatures wholly dependent on Christ and his grace—in the life-giving communion of the Triune God. In the words of John Meyendorff: "Man, while certainly a creature and, as such, *external* to God, is defined, in his very *nature*, as being fully himself only when he is in *communion* with God."[42] Drawing on the language of glorification in Romans 8:30, Leo the Great observes: "He united humanity to himself in such a way that he remained God, unchangeable. He imparted divinity to human beings in such a way that he did not destroy, but enriched them, by glorification."[43]

41 *Opus.* 7; trans. Cooper, *The Body in St. Maximus the Confessor,* 157.

42 *Byzantine Theology,* 225. Eric Mascall (*The Importance of Being Human,* 61–62) lucidly expresses the creaturely result of our deification: "Supernature simply means nature supernaturalized by grace, and the possibility of this supernaturalization lies in the openness of nature to God. . . . The more supernaturalized, the more truly natural it becomes. And all this because openness to God is of its very essence; dependence upon him is part of its definition."

43 *Serm.* 91. 2; Freeland, 384.

We are left with the question: What then does the elevation and glorification of our nature actually entail? Rowan Williams offers a helpful conceptual distinction between two ways that deification has been understood in the Christian tradition.[44] The first is the communication of divine attributes to human beings through participation in Christ, in a way suited to our nature and its glorification (e.g., eternal life and incorruptibility). The second is the creature's participation in the intra-divine relationship itself, the communion of love shared by the Father, Son, and Spirit. These are, of course, inseparable. It is by virtue of our participation in the life of the Trinitarian God that we partake of the divine attributes in a way suited to our nature.

The following selections, ancient and contemporary, state with particular eloquence the positive content of our deification. In the end, it is the language of divine life and love that must serve to express what it means to become "partakers of the divine nature." First is a selection from Maximus the Confessor on how the whole human being, body and soul, will in the end be deified in Christ by grace:

> The fullness of God permeates them wholly as the soul permeates the body. . . . He gives them life, not the life that comes from breathing air, nor that of veins coursing with blood, but the life that comes from being wholly infused with the fullness of God. God becomes to the soul (and through the soul to the body) what the soul is to the body, as God alone knows, so that the soul receives changelessness and the body immortality; hence the whole man, as the object of divine action, is divinized by being made God by the grace of God who became man.[45]

Thomas Aquinas presents the goal of participation in the divine life as nothing less than the enjoyment of God himself for those made in his image—and for Aquinas enjoyment of God is always defined by charity:

> A man adopts someone as his son forasmuch as out of goodness he admits him as heir to his estate. Now God is infinitely good: for which reason he admits his creatures to a participation of good

[44] "Deification," in *A Dictionary of Christian Spirituality*, ed. Gordon S. Wakefield (London: SCM Press, 1983), 106–8.

[45] *Amb.* 7; trans. Wilken, *On the Cosmic Mystery of Jesus Christ*, 63.

> things; especially rational creatures, who forasmuch as they are made to the image of God, are capable of divine beatitude. And this consists in the enjoyment of God, by which also God himself is happy and rich in himself—that is, in the enjoyment of himself.[46]

Speaking from the Western tradition, Eric Mascall expresses the profound mystery of our creaturely entrance into God's own mode of life through the incarnate Son of God:

> There the matter might have remained, had not God decided to do some even greater things for us, namely to give us the means of being incorporated into the human nature which the Son assumed, so that we should not be merely bathed in a radiance poured upon us from without but be taken up into its very source. By incorporation into Christ we become sons of God by adoption. The sonship which was imparted to his own individual human nature by the Incarnation is imparted to us by our incorporation into him. Thus the grace which the Christian receives, while it elevates him into the life of God and, in the scriptural phrase, makes him "a partaker of the divine nature" (2 Pet 1:4), does this by the specific means of communicating to him, by his incorporation into Christ, the sonship which the Son of God enjoys in the Holy Trinity. We become sons in the Son.[47]

Finally, Kenneth Paul Wesche, writing from the Eastern tradition, speaks of our deification as entrance into the Trinitarian communion:

> Union with God is the goal of *theosis* and the content of salvation. . . . *Theosis* is the mystery of human nature's perfection, not its alteration or destruction, because *theosis* is the mystery of eternal life in communion with God in the divine Logos and communion with God in the divine Logos is the very essence of human being as "created in the image and likeness of God."[48]

It remains beyond us, though, to express in a definitive way the precise results of deification for our creaturely nature and for commun-

46 *Summa theologiae* III, q. 23, a. 1.

47 *Christ, the Christian and the Church,* 100.

48 "Eastern Orthodox Spirituality: Union with God in *Theosis,*" 29, 31.

ion with the Triune God. Theology can and must clear away obstacles to right understanding, but we quickly pass from the language of description to the language of confession, and finally come to the border where even the language of confession must fall mute. Augustine wisely reminds us of this: "That he should make men gods is to be understood in divine silence."[49] We cannot yet see or comprehend all that the Father has in store for us in Christ through the Spirit.

> See what love the Father has given us, that we should be called children of God; and so we are. . . . Beloved, we are God's children now; it does not yet appear what we shall be, but we know that when he appears we shall be like him, for we shall see him as he is (1 Jn 3:1–2).

[49] C. Adim. 93 .2: *"Ut deos homines faciat, divino est intelligenda silentio"*; trans. Russell, *The Doctrine of Deification,* 332.

CHAPTER SIX

Conclusion: The Warrant for Christian Deification

For [Christ] did not love them to the point of their being gods by nature, nor to the point that they would be united to God so as to form one person with him. But he did love them up to a similar point: he loved them to the extent that they would be gods by their participation in grace— "I say you are gods"—(Ps 82:6)*; "He has granted to us precious and very great promises, that through these you may become partakers of the divine nature."* (2 Pet 1:4)

—Thomas Aquinas, *In Io.* 15:9–13

THE MEANING OF CHRISTIAN DEIFICATION

THIS STUDY began with the recognition that the Christian doctrine of deification (or divinization) needs explaining. What ground have we gained toward this end? The foundation for understanding deification is the redemption of our humanity in Christ himself through the "graced exchange" at the heart of the Gospel. By means of the assumption of human nature by the eternal Son of God, and the transformation of that nature in himself, we are called and enabled to participate as creatures in the divine nature (2 Pet 1:4). The Son of God became the Son of Man, so that the sons and daughters of men might become the sons and daughters of God. The Incarnation, passion, death, resurrection, and ascension of Christ remain the irreplaceable center of Christian deification. We can become "sons" and "gods" only in the one who is the true Son of God.

Though Christ redeemed the whole of our nature in himself, each of us is called to personally and freely appropriate that redemption. A fundamental premise of Christian deification is that human beings can be deified only through God's direct agency, only through having God himself dwelling effectively within them. It is principally through the indwelling of the Holy Spirit in baptism, and participation in Christ's body and blood in the Eucharist, that God himself comes to live effectively within us. And the goal of this indwelling is that we become progressively "conformed to the image of Christ" (Rom 8:29) and "transformed into the same image" through the Spirit (2 Cor 3:18). By his grace at work in us, our freedom is revived and strengthened, enabling us to work with him in our own transformation and to reach the goal of maturity in Christ. Through prayer and a life of Christian asceticism our communion with the Triune God is deepened and our likeness to Christ grows. Our progress in deification always follows a baptismal and Eucharistic pattern. The door by which we enter is also the way that we must walk. True progress in deification will always be marked by an ever deeper participation in the suffering, death, and resurrection of Christ (2 Cor 4:10–12).

We have also seen that deification does not mean an ontological promotion to something other than we are (that is, human beings made in God's image and likeness). We do not become God as God is, but we come to participate in his divine life and power. Our nature is elevated and glorified, but *as deified* we remain creatures and human beings completely dependent on God as our source. Deification is the honored status that God intended for us as his sons and daughters, a status forfeited in Adam and attained in Christ, the New Adam. Through our real incorporation into Christ we experience the fruits of divine life in a way suited to our nature, and we share in the Trinitarian fellowship of love: "that you may have fellowship with us; and our fellowship is with the Father and with his Son Jesus Christ" (1 Jn 1:3).

Biblical Foundation

Three guiding convictions, identified at the start, have governed this study. The first is that the Christian doctrine of deification is and must be biblically grounded. As is plain from their writings, the Fathers of the Church who first employed the concept of deification to describe our redemption in Christ believed that they were conveying what the Scriptures revealed. Whether or not one agrees with the interpretations that they offered (and that are summarized below), it is difficult to deny that they were attempting to give an accurate and comprehensive rendering of the biblical witness to our inheritance in Christ. A brief catalogue will help to recall the biblical foundations we have found for central aspects of Christian deification.

- The formula of exchange ("the Son of God became the Son of Man, so that the sons of men might become the sons of God") is anchored in the exchange Paul speaks of in 2 Corinthians 8:9.
- The centrality of divine filiation—of becoming "sons of God"—is found in both Paul and John (Gal 4:4–6; Rom 8:14–17, 29; 1 Jn 3:1–2).
- The notion of becoming "gods" is rooted in a Christological interpretation of Psalm 82:6 (Jn 10:34–35), and our vocation to be "partakers of the divine nature" is directly stated in 2 Peter 1:4.
- The conviction of the Church Fathers that baptism and the Eucharist are the primary means of the effective indwelling of God is found, inter alia, in Titus 3:5–7; 1 Corinthians 6:11, 19; Galatians 3:26–27; John 3:3–8; 1 Corinthians 10:16–17; and John 6:51–59.
- The goal of our redemption as conformity to Christ and transformation into his image is described by Paul (Rom 8:29; 2 Cor 3:18); the New Testament teaching on maturity (Mt 5:48; Heb 5:14, 6:1; 1 Cor 14:20; Col 1:28; Eph 4:13; Jas 1:4) and growth in virtue (2 Pet 1:5–8; Rom 13:12–14; Gal 5:19–24; Eph 4:17–32; Col 3:5–17) provides the content of what it means to be transformed into the image of Christ.
- Deification as including ongoing participation in the death and resurrection of Christ is attested by Paul (2 Cor 4:10–12; Phil 3:7–11; Rom 8:17).
- The use of the concept of participation by the Fathers is grounded in and confirmed by the biblical description of our redemption in Christ in terms of participation and sharing (Heb 2:14; 2 Pet 1:4; Heb 6:4; 2 Cor 13:13; Phil 2:1; 1 Cor 10:14–22).

Finally, the overarching biblical narrative for the doctrine of deification is Christ as the New Adam. It is no accident that in Irenaeus we find both a rich elaboration of Christ as the Second Adam and the beginnings of the doctrine of deification. In a sense, the doctrine of deification is a biblically and doctrinally rich elaboration of what Paul states as our destiny in 1 Corinthians 15:47: "Just as we have borne the image of the man of dust, we shall also bear the image of the man of heaven."

PATRISTIC TESTIMONY AND CONTEMPORARY REENGAGEMENT

The second guiding conviction is that the Christian doctrine of deification is at the patristic root of both the Eastern and Western theological traditions. Perhaps the most notable finding of this study is that the teaching on deification can be found not only in the Fathers of the East, but also widely in the Fathers of the West.[1] In order to show this broad agreement, I have at several points gathered together selections from authors East and West to show their striking similarity on the essentials (not necessarily on the details) of deification.[2] Their testimony speaks for itself. One might ask, however, whether the selections have been unjustifiably removed from their original settings and made to agree in the context of a predetermined framework of my own making. In answer, the outline of the doctrine of deification I have adopted here was gained by reading widely and deeply in the patristic texts in the first place. The framework slowly emerged as I read the Fathers in their own contexts and on their own terms. I then joined together key selections in the conviction that the Fathers do give a remarkable witness to a common understanding of our redemption in Christ. Their voices may not always be on the same pitch, but they are normally in the same key and in harmony with one another.

---

1 The notable absence from this broad agreement among the Fathers is Theodore of Mopsuestia and those closely identified with his theological and exegetical approach. Theodore represents only a particular strand of the Antiochene Fathers (his close friend John Chrysostom does not share his orientation). Donald Fairbairn, *Grace and Christology in the Early Church,* argues persuasively that Theodore is the exception to the patristic testimony on deification and grace.

2 For the particular and distinctive aspects of the individual Fathers on the doctrine of deification, see Russell, *The Doctrine of Deification.*

This conclusion regarding the Western Fathers and deification can now be advanced one step further: An understanding of Christian life as deification can also be found in significant later authors of the Western theological tradition. No one denies that the Byzantine tradition in the East has maintained and developed the patristic legacy, resulting in what we call today the Eastern doctrine of *theosis*. What we have also found is that the patristic notion of deification finds lively expression in Thomas Aquinas, who not only lays claim to being the most significant Western medieval theologian, but who was also the most important carrier of the patristic heritage to the post-Tridentine era in the West. He not only employs the characteristic vocabulary of deification, but more importantly he expresses and develops what we have identified as the *content* of the patristic account of deification. To rediscover the doctrine of deification, the West need not look only to the Greek Fathers (which is essential); a key part of the rediscovery is recognizing that a rich account of human deification in Christ is also present in the Western Fathers and Aquinas.

As we have seen, aspects of deification can also be found in the writings of key Protestant Reformers and theologians (Martin Luther, John Calvin, John Wesley), and many in the Protestant world are calling for a retrieval of the idea of salvation as deification. One such example is the plea by Reformed theologian T. F. Torrance for a reengagement with the patristic notion of *theosis*:

> At this point let me plead for a reconsideration by the Reformed Church of what the Greek fathers called *theosis*. This is usually unfortunately translated *deification*, but it has nothing to do with the *divinization* of man any more than the Incarnation has to do with the humanization of God. *Theosis* was the term the Fathers used to emphasize the fact that through the Spirit we have to do with God in his utter sublimity, his sheer Godness or holiness; creatures though we are, men on earth, in the Spirit we are made to participate in the saving acts that are abruptly and absolutely divine, election, adoption, regeneration or sanctification and we participate in them by grace alone. *Theosis* describes man's involvement in such a mighty act of God upon him that he is raised up to find the true centre of his existence not in himself but in Holy God, where he lives

> and moves and has his being in the uncreated but creative energy of the Holy Spirit. By *theosis* the Greek fathers wished to express the fact that in the new coming of the Holy Spirit we are up against *God* in the most absolute sense, God in his ultimate holiness or Godness.[3]

Torrance appears to be operating under the impression that this account of our participation in God is found solely in the Greek Fathers—we have seen that it is in the Latin Fathers as well. And though he rejects the terms "deification" and "divinization," he curiously welcomes the term "*theosis,*" which is simply the Greek word coined by Gregory of Nazianzus to mean "deification." What Torrance presumably dislikes about the terms "deification," "divinization," and "humanization" is that (in his judgment) they violate the proper distinction between the creature and the Creator in the Christian account of salvation.[4] What I have attempted to show in this study is that an accurate account of deification in the Christian tradition, East and West, upholds the proper distinction between creature and Creator on the one hand, and on the other guarantees the kind of direct and intimate participation of the creature with God that Torrance praises. As Christians today seek from within their various confessional traditions to reengage the doctrine of deification, it is crucial that the full testimony to deification, East and West, be recovered and rightly understood.

EMBEDDED WITHIN CHRISTIAN DOCTRINE

The third conviction guiding this study is that an account of deification must be firmly embedded within Christian doctrine. It cannot stand alone, nor should it be understood as replacing or superseding other Christian doctrines. As stated previously, it is a summary term for all that God intends for us in Christ through the Spirit. The pattern set by Athanasius—one of the foremost proponents of deification—points the way for us:

---

3 *Theology in Reconstruction* (Grand Rapids, MI: Eerdmans, 1965), 243.

4 For Torrance's understanding of *theosis* more generally, see Myk Habets, "Reforming Theōsis," in *Theōsis: Deification in Christian Theology*, 146–67.

> Adoption, renewal, salvation, sanctification, grace, transcendence, illumination, and vivification are all presented [by Athanasius] as equivalents to deification. Although the concept [of deification] itself is not controversial, Athanasius may well be intending to exclude any possibility of misunderstanding.[5]

For the same reason (that is, to avoid misunderstanding) deification today needs to be embedded within Christian truth and explained by reference to other doctrines. It requires the fertile soil of creedal confession. Historically, the doctrine of deification developed as a way to express more profoundly the truth as revealed in the Scriptures, as a deeper intuition of what God has in store for us in Christ through the Spirit. As a kind of capstone to Christian truth, it is best served by continuing to be embedded within classical Christian doctrine.

To put this in other terms, the Christian understanding of deification is not a novel discovery, an exotic theological fad, or some kind of new passageway to God distinct from a more traditional Christian approach. It does not describe a vague and generalized union of the human with the divine. Rather, it depends entirely on the specific confession of the Triune God, the Incarnation of the eternal Son, and the gift of the indwelling Holy Spirit in the Church. It finds its place in Christian practice: in the sacraments, in Christian asceticism, and in prayer. It is located within the eschatological tension of Christian existence. The process of deification is already begun in us, but it is not yet complete. Deification is especially closely related to our adoption and regeneration as sons and daughters of God. As Andrew Louth says, "The doctrine of deification is the deepest implication of our taking seriously the doctrine of adoption."[6] If Christians today desire to recapture and promote the idea of deification in the Church, then this must be done within the context of Christian confession and practice.

---

[5] Russell, *The Doctrine of Deification,* 177. Kärkkäinen, *One with God,* 31, makes this point more generally: "Terms such as transformation, union, participation, partaking, intermingling, elevation, interpenetration, transmutation, commingling, assimilation, reintegration, adoption, recreation are used to refer to the same reality [i.e. deification]."

[6] "Manhood into God," 73.

THE WARRANT FOR CHRISTIAN DEIFICATION

At the beginning of this study several key questions were identified that are often lodged against the doctrine of deification. Most have been answered en route, but it will be helpful to summarize here the answers given. First, there is convincing evidence that Christian deification is not correctly understood as an importation from Greek thought foreign to Christian faith. Rather, the terminology of deification was first employed to describe a specifically biblical account of our adoptive sonship in Christ through the Spirit. Second, the doctrine of deification does not enhance or magnify the place of the Incarnation to the detriment of Christ's atoning work on the Cross. As we observed, the Incarnation for the Fathers is the inauguration of one united work that encompasses the whole of Christ's life, passion, death, resurrection, and ascension. When the Christian tradition uses the formula of exchange, the Cross and the atoning work of Christ are understood as essential. Third, deification does not compromise the fundamental distinction between God and the created order, but sustains and requires that distinction. By means of the concept of participation, deification upholds at one and the same time the infinite difference between God and creation and the close communion God intends to have with us, his creatures.

This leaves us with the final question regarding the warrant for the doctrine of deification. Even if we grant that the doctrine of deification does not suffer from the defects sometimes ascribed to it, does it add anything to our grasp of the saving work of God in Christ? Is it really useful? Given the real possibility of misunderstanding, it is warranted?

The fourth-century controversy concerning the use of the term *homoousios* ("consubstantial," "one in being") provides a potential parallel for us. Inserted into the Creed of Nicaea in 325 to rule out the position of Arius that the Son was a creature, the word *homoousios* was then hotly disputed in the ensuing period (roughly from 350 to 380). Some objected that the term was not biblical. Others justly complained that *homoousios* had overtones from gnostic usage (implying that God had parts), and that some leaders in the Church were interpreting *homoousios* to exclude the personal distinction of the Son from the Father. Athanasius and others championed the term, however, and provided intensive clarification on its proper meaning. In the end it was adopted because it ensured the truth of the Son's full and complete divinity and his personal distinction from the Father, as revealed in the Scriptures. The term *homoousios* made a significant contribution to the explication of Christian truth. But since its adoption it has remained firmly embedded in the basic creedal confession of faith (the Nicene Creed), where it finds its home and proper location. In a similar way, this study has attempted to give "intensive clarification" about the meaning of the term "deification." Though not found in the Bible, it has biblical roots and serves to explain biblical revelation. It is—and must remain—embedded within the confession of Christian truth.

What contribution does the idea of deification have to offer? What truths does it ensure and enhance? Deification ensures that our understanding of "sanctification" does not stop short at cleansing and purification from sin; that sanctification has as its end and goal communion with God himself brought about by his direct agency. It ensures that our understanding of salvation is nothing short of the union with God that we were created for, and that our creaturely destiny is found in direct relationship with the eternal God—Father, Son and Holy Spirit.

Deification, rightly understood, sets us on a path that avoids both Pelagian self-sanctification and an idolatrous identification of ourselves with God. It rules out the former, because it is so clearly founded on divine initiative and indwelling. Human beings may be capable of deluding themselves that they can achieve virtue and godliness simply through the exercise of innate capacities. But deification closes the door to this idea by showing that our end and goal is to be "gods" and "sons of God," and to participate in the life of God. There is no room here for making progress simply by some capacity within ourselves. Rather, we are to make use of all our capacities to cling to God and cooperate with him as he directs and transforms us from within, and leads us into full communion with himself. Deification deflects a Pelagian tendency, not by curbing the power of human freedom, but by exhibiting that our destiny in God is so clearly one that we could not even hope to attain by created capacities alone or by the exercise of our wills. Only God can deify, and so only God by his effective indwelling and grace can bring us to our true end.

A Christian account of deification also undercuts the tendency toward idolatry, toward making ourselves gods or identifying ourselves as God. Unlike Adam and Eve who succumbed to the temptation to become "like God" on their own terms, we become "sons of God" and "gods" only in Jesus Christ, the true Son and image of God. In deification, we are not enabled to become "gods" on our own and achieve equal status with God. Rather, we are called to be gods by *participating* in God himself, by being joined to the Incarnate Word through the Spirit. Accurately presented, deification reminds us that in Christ we remain the creatures that we are, and find our joy and delight in being elevated by sheer grace to communion with God and participation in his life and power.

Finally, the doctrine of deification enhances the doctrine of the Incarnation, and consequently of the Trinity and the divine economy of the Father in Christ through the Spirit. It reminds us that there is no bypassing the Incarnation or making it a temporary stage on the way to things higher. The Incarnate Word remains the central locus of our salvation and deification—and our creaturely participation in the divine life is always mediated by being in Christ and members of his body. We are "sons and daughters in the Son" and are deified to the degree that we are found in, and transformed into the image of, Christ himself. The primary warrant, then, for Christian deification is that it ensures and enhances the full biblical revelation of our call: to become sons and daughters formed in the image of Christ; to be temples of the Holy Spirit and members of the household of God; to live in direct and eternal communion with the Father through the Son and in the Holy Spirit.

> "What no eye has seen, nor ear heard, nor the human heart conceived, what God has prepared for those who love him"—these things God has revealed to us through the Spirit. (1 Cor 2:9–10, NRSV)
>
> Now to him who by the power at work within us is able to accomplish abundantly far more than all we can ask or imagine, to him be glory in the church and in Christ Jesus to all generations, forever and ever. Amen. (Eph 3:20–21, NRSV)

Select Bibliography of Secondary Sources

Allchin, A. M. *Participation in God: A Forgotten Strand in Anglican Tradition.* Wilton, CT: Morehouse-Barlow, 1988.

Aulén, Gustaf. *Christus Victor,* trans. A. G. Herbert. London: SPCK, 1970.

Balás, David L. *ΜΕΤΟΥΣΙΑ ΘΕΟΥ: Man's Participation in God's Perfection according to St. Gregory of Nyssa.* Rome: Herder, 1966.

Balthasar, Hans Urs von. *The Glory of the Lord: A Theological Aesthetics,* vol. 7, trans. Brian McNeil. Edinburgh: T&T Clark, 1989.

———. *Credo: Meditations on the Apostles' Creed,* trans. David Kipp. New York: Crossroad, 1990

———. *Theo-Drama: Theological Dramatic Theory,* vol. 4, trans. Graham Harrison. San Francisco, CA: Ignatius Press, 1994.

Behr, John. *The Nicene Faith,* 2 parts. Crestwood, NY: St. Vladimir's Press, 2004.

Bouyer, Louis. *The Christian Mystery: From Pagan Myth to Christian Mysticism,* trans. I. Trethowan. Edinburgh: T&T Clark, 1989.

Bonner, Gerald. "Augustine's Conception of Deification." *Journal of Theological Studies* New Series 37 (1986): 360–86.

Braaten, Carl E., and Robert W. Jenson, eds. *Union with Christ: The New Finnish Interpretation of Luther.* Grand Rapids, MI: Eerdmans, 1998.

Burghardt, Walter J. *The Image of God in Man according to Cyril of Alexandria.* Washington, DC: Catholic University Press, 1957.

Byrnes, Michael. *Conformation to the Death of Christ and the Hope of Resurrection: An Exegetico-Theological Study of 2 Corinthians 4:7–15 and Philippians 3:7–11.* Rome: Editrice Pontificia Università Gregoriana, 2003.

Charles, J. Daryl. *Virtue Amidst Vice: The Catalog of Virtues in 2 Peter 1,* JSNT Suppl. 150. Sheffield: Sheffield Academic Press, 1997.

Christensen, Michael J. "Theosis and Sanctification: John Wesley's Reformulation of a Patristic Doctrine." *Wesleyan Theological Journal* 31 (1996): 71–94.

Clark, Stephen B. *Redeemer: Understanding the Meaning of the Life, Death, and Resurrection of Jesus Christ.* Ann Arbor, MI: Servant, 1992.

———. *Catholics and the Eucharist.* Ann Arbor, MI: Servant, 2000.

Congar, Yves. "La déification dans le tradition spirituelle de l'Orient." *La vie spirituelle* 43 (1935): suppl., 91–107.

———. *The Mystery of the Temple,* trans. Reginald Trevett. Westminster: Newman Press, 1962.

———. *I Believe in the Holy Spirit,* trans. David Smith. New York: Crossroad, 1997.

Cooper, Adam G. *The Body in St. Maximus the Confessor: Holy Flesh, Wholly Deified.* Oxford: Oxford University Press, 2005.

Dauphinais, Michael, and Matthew Levering. *Holy People, Holy Land: A Theological Introduction to the Bible.* Grand Rapids, MI: Brazos, 2005.

De Lubac, Henri. *Medieval Exegesis,* vol. 1: *The Four Senses of Scripture,* trans. Marc Sebanc. Grand Rapids, MI: Eerdmans, 1998.

Drewery, Benjamin. "Deification." In *Christian Spirituality: Essays in Honour of Gordon Rupp,* ed. Peter Brooks. London: SCM Press, 1975, 33–62.

Fairbairn, Donald. *Grace and Christology in the Early Church.* Oxford: Oxford University Press, 2003.

Finch, Jeffrey. "Irenaeus on the Christological Basis of Human Divinization," in *Theōsis: Deification in Christian Theology,* ed. Stephen Finlan and Vladimir Kharlamov. Eugene, OR: Pickwick Publications, 2006, 86–103.

Finlan, Stephen, and Vladimir Kharlamov. *Theōsis: Deification in Christian Theology.* Eugene, OR: Pickwick Publications, 2006.

Glazov, Gregory. "Theōsis, Judaism, and Old Testament Anthropology," in *Theōsis: Deification in Christian Theology,* ed. Stephen Finlan and Vladimir Kharlamov. Eugene, OR: Pickwick Publication, 2006, 16–31.

Gross, Jules. *La divinisation du chrétien d'après les Pères grecs.* Paris: Gabalda, 1938; English translation: *The Divinization of the Christian according to the Greek Fathers,* trans. Paul A. Onica. Anaheim: A & C Press, 2002.

Habets, Myk. "Reforming Theōsis," in *Theōsis: Deification in Christian Theology,* eds. Stephen Finlan and Vladimir Kharlamov. Eugene, OR: Pickwick Publications, 2006, 146–47.

Hallonsten, Gösta. "*Theosis* in Recent Research: A Renewal of Interest and a Need for Clarity." In *Partakers of the Divine Nature: The History and Development of Deification in the Christian Traditions,* eds. Michael J. Christensen and Jeffrey A. Wittung (Madison/Teaneck, NJ: Fairleigh Dickinson University Press, 2007), 281–93.

Harnack, Adolph. *History of Dogma,* vol. 2, trans. Neil Buchanan. Gloucester, MA: Peter Smith, 1976.

Hart, David Bentley. *The Beauty of the Infinite: The Aesthetics of Christian Truth.* Grand Rapids, MI: Eerdmans, 2003.

Heron, Alasdair. *The Holy Spirit: The Holy Spirit in the Bible, in the History of Christian Thought and in Recent Theology.* London: Marshall, Morgan and Scott, 1983.

Hooker, Morna D. "Interchange in Christ." *Journal of Theological Studies,* New Series 22 (1971): 349–61.

Kärkkäinen, Veli-Matti. *One With God: Salvation as Deification and Justification.* Collegeville, MN: Liturgical Press, 2004.

Keating, Daniel A. "The Baptism of Jesus in Cyril of Alexandria: The Re-Creation of the Human Race." *Pro Ecclesia* 8 (1999): 201–22.

———. *The Appropriation of Divine Life in Cyril of Alexandria.* Oxford: Oxford University Press, 2004.

———. "Justification, Sanctification and Divinization in Thomas Aquinas." In *Aquinas on Doctrine: A Critical Introduction,* ed. Thomas Weinandy, Daniel Keating, and John Yocum. London: Continuum/T&T Clark, 2004, 139–58.

Kelly, J. N. D. *Early Christian Doctrines,* rev. ed. Peabody, MA: Prince Press, 2003.

Kerr, Fergus. *After Aquinas: Versions of Thomism.* Oxford: Blackwell, 2002.

Kittel, G. "εἰκών," in *Theological Dictionary of the New Testament,* ed. idem, trans. Geoffrey Bromiley. Grand Rapids, MI: Eerdmans, 1964, 381–97.

Kolp, A. L. "Partakers of the Divine Nature: The Use of II Pet. 1:4 by Athanasius." *Studia Patristica* 17 (1982): 1018–23.

Levering, Matthew. *Christ's Fulfillment of Torah and Temple: Salvation according to Thomas Aquinas.* Notre Dame, IN: University of Notre Dame Press, 2002.

Lossky, Vladimir. *In the Image and Likeness of God.* Crestwood, NY: St. Vladimir's Press, 1974.

———. *The Mystical Theology of the Eastern Church.* Cambridge: James Clarke, 1991.

Louth, Andrew. "Manhood into God: The Oxford Movement, The Fathers and the Deification of Man." In *Essays Catholic and Radical*, ed. Kenneth Leech and Rowan Williams. London: Bowerdean, 1983, 70–80.

Maloney, George A. *The Undreamed Has Happened: God Lives within Us.* Scranton: University of Scranton Press, 2003.

Mantzaridis, G. I. *The Deification of Man: St. Gregory Palamas and the Orthodox Tradition,* trans. Liadain Sherrard. Crestwood, NY: St. Vladimir's Press, 1984.

Marsh, Thomas. *The Triune God.* Dublin: Columba, 1994.

Mascall, E. L. *Christ, the Christian and the Church: A Study of the Incarnation and its Consequences.* London: Longmans, Green and Co., 1946.

———. *The Importance of Being Human: Some Aspects of The Christian Doctrine of Man.* London: Oxford University Press, 1959.

McCormick, Steve K. "Theosis in Chrysostom and Wesley: An Eastern Paradigm on Faith and Love." *Wesleyan Theological Journal* 26 (1991): 38–103.

Meyendorff, John. *Byzantine Theology.* New York: Fordham University Press, 1974.

Mosser, Carl. "The Greatest Possible Blessing: Calvin and Deification." *Scottish Journal of Theology* 55 (2002): 36–57.

———. "The Earliest Patristic Interpretation of Psalm 82, Jewish Antecedents, and the Origins of Christian Deification." *Journal of Theological Studies* New Series 56 (2005): 30–74.

Nellas, P. *Deification in Christ: Perspectives on the Nature of the Human Person,* trans. Norman Russell. Crestwood, NY: St. Vladimir's Press, 1987.

Newman, John Henry. *Lectures on Justification,* 6th ed. London: Longmans, Green, and Co., 1892.

———. "The Indwelling Spirit." In *Parochial and Plain Sermons,* vol. 2, 19. San Francisco, CA: Ignatius, 1987, 363–72.

Norris, F. W. "Deification: Consensual and Cogent." *Scottish Journal of Theology* 49 (1996): 411–28.

Orthodox Spirituality: An Outline of the Orthodox Ascetical and Mystical Tradition, 3rd ed. Crestwood, NY: St. Vladimir's Press, 1987.

Pinckaers, Servais. *The Sources of Christian Ethics,* trans. Sr. Mary Thomas Noble. Edinburgh: T&T Clark, 1995.

Rakestraw, Robert V. "Becoming like God: An Evangelical Doctrine of Theosis." *Journal of Evangelical Theology* 40 (1997): 257–69.

Ratzinger, Joseph (Pope Benedict XVI). *Dogma and Preaching,* trans. Matthew J. O'Connell. Chicago, IL: Franciscan Herald Press, 1985.

Rogerson, J. W. "The Hebrew Conception of Corporate Personality: A Re-Examination." *Journal of Theological Studies* New Series 21 (1970): 1–16.

Russell, Norman. "Partakers of the Divine Nature (2 Pet. 1:4) in the Byzantine Tradition." In *Kathegetria: Essays presented to Joan Hussey*, ed. J. Chrysostomides. Camberley: Porphyrogenitus, 1988, 51–67.

———. *The Doctrine of Deification in the Greek Patristic Tradition.* Oxford: Oxford University Press, 2004.

Smith, Daniel A. "Irenaeus and the Baptism of Jesus." *Theological Studies* 58 (1997): 618–42.

Stavropoulos, Christoforos. *Partakers of the Divine Nature,* trans. Stanley Harakas. Minneapolis: Light and Life, 1976.

Studer, Basil. "Divinization." In *Encyclopedia of the Early Church*, vol. 1, ed. Angelo Di Berardino, trans. Adrian Walford. New York: Oxford University Press, 1992.

Torrance, T. F. *Theology in Reconstruction.* Grand Rapids, MI: Eerdmans, 1965.

Ware, Kallistos. *The Orthodox Church.* London: Penguin, 1964.

———. "Salvation and Theosis in Orthodox Theology." In *Luther et la réforme allemande dans une perspective oecuménique*, ed. W. Schneemelcher. Geneva: Éditions du Centre Orthodoxe, 1983, 167–84.

Weinandy, Thomas G. "St. Irenaeus and the *Imago Dei.*" *Logos* 6 (2003): 15–34.

Wesche, Kenneth Paul. "Eastern Orthodox Spirituality: Union with God in *Theosis.*" *Theology Today* 56 (1999): 29–43.

Williams, A. N. *The Ground of Union: Deification in Aquinas and Palamas.* Oxford: Oxford University Press, 1999.

Williams, Rowan. "Deification." In *A Dictionary of Christian Spirituality*, ed. Gordon S. Wakefield. London: SCM Press, 1983, 106–8.

Yocum, John P. "Sacraments in Aquinas." In *Aquinas on Doctrine: A Critical Introduction*, ed. Thomas Weinandy, Daniel Keating, and John Yocum. London: Continuum/T&T Clark, 2004, 159–81.

Young, Frances. *Nicaea to Chalcedon.* London: SCM Press, 1983.

Zizioulas, John. *Being as Communion.* Crestwood, NY: St. Vladimir's Press, 1985.

General Index

Index of Scripture References